MR. BEVERLEY C. DUER
255 UNION STREET
SAN FRANCISCO 11, CALIF.

MR. BEVERLEY C. DUER
255 UNION STREET
SAN FRANCISCO 11, CALIF.

The Story of American Yachting

134

The Story of

American Yachting

TOLD IN PICTURES

with photographs by

MORRIS ROSENFELD

and text by

William H. Taylor and Stanley Rosenfeld

APPLETON · CENTURY · CROFTS, Inc., NEW YORK

ACC (1)

To those who have created,

recorded and preserved

the written and visual picture

of the heritage

of American yachting.

Foreword

WITHIN the past few years millions of Americans have found a new interest and recreation in the sport of yachting. The innovations and changes of the times are directly reflected in the design and types of craft that are popular now, but the emotional appeals that attract so many new yachtsmen today are very much the same as they were a hundred years ago. There are some differences. Compact and powerful new engines have brought the thrill of high speed to the waters. Speed is a relative sensation, however, and in the last century, when all of life moved at a more leisurely pace, a sailboat scudding before a spanking breeze must have been a thrill to the most adventuresome. On the other hand, the day of the great sailing yachts, a topmast towering fifteen stories over her deck, and 16,000 square feet of sail spread to the wind, seems to be a thing of the past, along with the particular sensation of power known by those who sailed her.

It is hoped that for the new lovers of the sport, as well as the veteran sailor, the pages of this book will provide some general picture of the heritage of American yachting. The first section deals with the emotional appeal of yachting, a human factor that remains relatively constant. The second is devoted to the historical development of the yachts themselves. The story of the America's Cup, the most dramatic racing series and the one with the longest history, is told in the third. Ocean racing, the most challenging of sailing events, is pictured in the fourth. The fifth reflects the rapidly expanding contemporary yachting scene.

There are over two hundred thousand photographs in the Rosenfeld file, and thousands of others were looked at in the course of research in museums and libraries. A great number of them, for historical reasons or pure nostalgia, might have been included in these pages if it had been possible. The selection of those that do appear was determined by their historical significance and emotional appeal, conditioned as the book took a form and integrity of its own, by the relationship of the illustrations to each other, and to the sequence of the story.

Each wave that rolls upon the shore is different than the one before; and each person finds in yachting some experience unique to him. These pages are aimed at the broad panorama of the yachting story as well as the specific details that lend perspective. Rare and startling moments have their singular quality because of their contrast with the usual and routine. All ocean racing need not be a dramatic fight against the elements. On many days the sea can be a very quiet and mannerly lady. The choice of illustrations in this book tried to reflect the moods of sailors and the sea as well as the historical continuity of the story of yachting.

STANLEY ROSENFELD

Contents

The Story of American Yachting

1

1

WHY PEOPLE
GO YACHTING

Why People Go Yachting

IN warm weather, the mere presence of a body of water is an invitation. To a small boy a puddle in the road is so alluring he just has to step into it. A baby splashing in the bath, children romping at the beach or a man standing on the shore, all respond instinctively to the lure of the water. It's a call that beckons well over twenty million Americans down to the water and into more than five million assorted craft. The "wonders in the deep," in biblical times a baffling mystery to the few who came in contact with them, have become a part of the way of life for a great many of us.

One of the reasons for the mass movement to the waters is our geography. There is a wonderful variety of natural and man-made waterways available to all parts of the country. With the general increase in leisure and wealth, and the basic interest of all people in recreation, it is only logical

that more and more of them should find their relaxation afloat. The present boom in yachting is reflected in newspapers, magazines, TV programs, and the number of books on sailing. In this do-it-yourself age, most of the stories deal with ways of getting afloat, and the types of boats and equipment available. Even in its advertising, the boating industry has been content with providing information on its products, with little attempt at high-pressure selling of boating in general, or motivation through emotional appeal. It would almost seem that the reasons for getting afloat are so well known that they hardly need be mentioned.

Other industries outside the boating field —clothing, linen, tobacco, and beverage— use yachting scenes to create impressions of coolness, cleanliness, excitement, and refreshment. They are obvious and generally accepted ideas. One of the appeals of sail-

ing, however, is that it has so much more to offer the heart, mind, and hands. In an age when all a man's senses are pounded by sensational newspaper headlines, TV terror tales and the imminent threat of ultimate disaster, yachting offers freedom, and a clean, sharp relief from the pressures of a mechanized world.

There are two particularly keen sensations of power afloat. One is personal, the other is felt by all. The boy with his hand on the tiller sailing his eight-foot pram, and the captain of the U.S.S. *United States* have an experience in common. It is the sense of power and authority that comes from command. It has been sought since the time of the first chieftain of the first tribal clan. Afloat, it is more than sheer power alone.

The squall can mean a fury of wind and a deluge of rain, but it can also clear the air of its humid discomfort, bringing new life into the atmosphere. Here a New York Thirty Footer pits itself against the weather.

In the Bible, in Genesis 18:19, the phrase "he will command" implied the responsibility of proper guidance as well as the authority of command. To this day, the captain of a vessel has the authority, as well as the responsibility, of properly guiding his ship. However abstract the idea may be, the feeling of command is intimate and direct, and afloat, the words "You're in command" have a depth of meaning and work a subtle wonder in boy and man alike.

The other power comes from a communion between the boat and those aboard. It is the feeling, particularly sharp when the going is rough, that between them they have the power of mastery over the elements. Straining shrouds, taut sheets and sails, and driving hull seem an extension of the bodies of the crew. The will to go seems to be in the boat as well as in them. In a motorboat, especially a fast one traveling into the wind and sea, the hull seems to leap from wave to wave and the surge of power is felt all through the body. When wind and wave are high, since the boat is bigger than the people in it, the communion between them so close and the mastery of the elements so real, the sailor intimately knows a strength greater than his own.

The sailor knows appeals to more bodily senses than the sense of power. There can be a tenseness to the sense of timing for a racing skipper when he crosses tacks with a rival craft. In that split second of concern, when he knows it is too late to cross the other boat's bow, he must decide whether to put the helm down and come about under her lee, or put the helm up and drive around her stern. The challenge to his skill in timing is one of the joys of racing, but a sailor is always making time in one way or another. He feels a sense of timing in his knees as they bend to meet the roll of the deck beneath him. He flexes to meet the leap of the hull over a cresting sea, or the pitch of the deck as a big wave comes up astern. In all his motions there is the timing and rhythm of a sort of nautical ballet, sometimes violent, sometimes gently swaying, often an unconscious movement, but, for a man, an exercise of grace and dignity in response to the timeless motion of moving water.

The sailor often knows time in its spatial quality. For those who sail on tidal waters, the ebb and flow of the tide provides an eternal clockwork and a variety of meanings. The salty tang of the beach at low tide can lend a heady fragrance to the an-

chorage, but it may mean that the dinghy rowed to the beach at high water and left there has to be hauled over a hundred yards of clammy mud before it can be floated. The sailor knows time as having vertical direction, for when his craft is moored to a dock, what at high tide was a level step to get ashore, a few hours later may mean a drop of ten feet to get back aboard. The tidewater sailor is also aware that time brings changes he cannot easily see, for the channel deep enough at high tide may be impassable at low.

Water is not the only element with a special rhythm for the sailor. The winds too, though sometimes variable, often are quite predictable. Along most ocean shores, the afternoon sea breeze is usually dependable. For the motorboatman to anticipate it may make the difference between a smooth, fast voyage or a slow, rough one. In a sailboat, the morning may mean drifting in a calm, the afternoon, heeling before a spanking breeze. Inland waters, under the influence of hills, plain or heat, have their own pattern of winds to please or confound the local sailor, and knowing that pattern well is one of his skills.

Another is knowing the motions peculiar to his boat. Different hull forms respond in different ways to the waves. The boat with a wide, flat transom will meet a following sea in a different way from a boat with a narrow stern. With a little experience, the man at the helm senses the motion of the boat, and almost instinctively provides the guidance she asks for. In effect, every boat has her own rhythm and timing, and a sea-kindly helmsman becomes a part of it. A practical application of the knowledge of how long and how far a boat will carry her way might make the difference between a smart landing at the yacht

A fine day to be sailing—*Mouette*, an English-built Twelve-Meter sloop, snores along on an easy reach with a good breeze and a smooth sea on Long Island Sound.

club dock, or a sloppy collision with it. If the audience on the club lawn is a critical one, the hurt to the skipper's pride might be as severe as the damage to his craft.

With a little cooperation, a boat can provide a wonderful sense of confidence in her crew. It probably is no more true for children than adults, but in watching children afloat it is much more apparent. There aren't too many places that help build a rugged individual any more. Afloat, in a situation that can really try a boy's independence at a level he can master, he can tend the tiller, trim a sheet or improvise a whisker pole. Aboard a boat, where all work together, the sense of fun, of being on a lark, is as true in a rowboat in a park lake as on a round-the-world cruise. On a small boat, though, from the moment one fellow casts off, and another steers away, there is the added sharing of responsibility and skill, as well as fun. And though within the confines of a small boat the crew must work closely together, just by being out under the open sky, and looking off over the distant water, a man can always feel somewhat alone. It is a pleasing paradox.

Some sailors are quickened by competition. Afloat, it can be broad and active or taut and precise. In a Saturday regatta, speed in setting the spinnaker, skill in trimming sheets or tending the helm, make it a match of man against man as well as boat against boat. Exhilaration may come not so much from the wind blowing against the body, spray flying in the sun, the angle of the deck challenging balance, or the lunging hull beneath, as from the chance of beating the other fellow, who has the same thought in mind, racing his craft a few yards off to leeward. In a long ocean race, the fleet may spread out, and in a few hours boats are over the horizon and out of sight of each other. Then, with the competition unseen and their position unknown, the race can go to the crew that can drive itself hardest, can be continually self-disciplined,

despite danger in storm, fatigue, or frustration in calm.

Power-boat men who like a test of precision in calculation have the predicted log race. This event is run over a course in which check points are designated, such as buoys, points of land or islands. Before the race, each navigator sends in to the race committee a precise schedule of his proposed passage over the course, with the exact time he expects to pass each check point. Once started, he can check his engine speed, but cannot look at a watch to check his progress. The winner is the navigator whose actual passage shows the least percentage of error to his predicted run. Despite variations in current and weather, the error is sometimes an amazingly small part of one per cent.

It is difficult to think of the waters without thinking of the weather. The violence of the wind can humble the greatest ocean liner, but its gentleness can breathe life into a gossamer sail. The squall can mean a fury of wind and a deluge of rain, but it can also clear the air of its humid discomfort, and spark new life into the atmosphere. Fog can bring dampness, isolation, the delicate tracery of the faint outlines of an anchorage, or the jangle of bells from boats anchored in a throughfare. Wind means action and flying spray. The sun means warmth, light, and just as sunset brings a riot of color, gold, coral and turquoise reflected in the water, so are all the aspects of the weather reflected in the spirits of the sailor.

Quite separate from all these stimulating aspects of the sport, there is an entirely different one—the opportunity for complete relaxation; for solitude if you desire it. The man whose business days are a hectic round of dealing with the public, answering the telephone, meeting emergencies, being day after day at the beck and call of his customers, his clients, his bosses; constantly making split-second decisions whose outcome

Afloat, in a situation that can really try a boy's independence at a level he can master, he can tend the
tiller, trim a sheet or improvise a whisker pole.

seriously affects his own or other people's welfare—for such a man, a boat may be a means of getting away from it all, for a day, a week, or a month.

If peace and quiet is his goal, the yachtsman can shove off when the opportunity offers and leave no phone number. Alone—if his boat is small enough to be within his powers to sail singlehanded—or with a few chosen companions, he can leave the crowd and the racket and the jangling bells far astern. He can enjoy a peaceful sail on a sunny day, or under a summer moon, and bring up at the end of it in a safe, calm harbor, away from the crowd, snug his ship down for the night, have a quiet pipe or two, and turn in.

He can get far enough away from the busier ports to enjoy solitude; to dig clams, fish for his supper off the boat, or stroll on the beach or in the woods of a lonely island. If he tires of this, he can put into a port where he knows he will find friends, ashore or in other boats like his, and enjoy their company. When it palls, all he need do is up-anchor, start his engine or make sail, and be off for other harbors or even for a

few days offshore, clear entirely of the land and its people.

It makes little difference whether he cruises in a motorboat or a sailboat. The sailing craft offers, to its devotees, more fun in the actual handling of the craft under conditions that are no two days alike, more skills to acquire, more satisfaction in the accomplishment of passages by making use of the forces of nature—the wind and tide. But the motorboat gives him a greater range of cruising grounds, farther from home if he is a big-city dweller; can take him to his favorite haunts quicker; can make him surer of getting home in time for work on Monday, if he must.

It is this sort of boating that appeals to the noncompetitive, reflective sort of sailor. It is a way of life he can enjoy for a weekend or a vacation, for a sabbatical year or, if he's reached retirement age, for the rest of his life if he likes. For there's no age limit to boating. You can enjoy it, in one or another of its forms, at any age from eight to eighty—and maybe a year or two beyond those limits either way, if circumstances permit.

Ghosting along in a sunset calm; a moment of peace and contentment afloat. This was George Granbery's sloop *Anita*, a successful boat in Long Island Sound overnight races as well as a fine one for this kind of sailing.

Ocean racing, with competition over the horizon, demands steady, skillful helmsmanship. Hours of it on end wear a man down. Here the helmsman will take his eye off the compass in a minute and look aloft to check the set of his sails.

There can be a tenseness to the sense of timing for a racing skipper when he crosses tacks with a rival craft. (In that split second of concern, when he knows it's too late to cross the other's bow, he must decide whether to put the helm down and come about under her lee or put the helm up and drive around her stern.) Here is a foul in the making. It looks as if No. 48 has put his helm down too late to tack safely to leeward of No. 41—and under the racing rules No. 41, on the starboard tack, has the right of way.

Fog brings dampness, isolation, the delicate tracery of the faint outline of an anchorage or the jangle of bells from boats anchored in a throughfare.

Beam to beam and spinnakers drawing perfectly—this is one of the tense moments of racing, where a break, or one momentary flaw in sail trimming or helmsmanship, means win or lose.

"Roll and go!" A schooner, her big genoa jib and fisherman staysail drawing in a strong breeze, gives a fine feeling of lift and power. This was *Yolu San,* reaching down Vineyard Sound, off Martha's Vineyard, Massachusetts, one day in 1936 in a smoky sou'wester.

After the tension of a race comes the relaxation in port, at its best when set to music. The musicians happen to be three of the sport's great ocean racing men—Chick Larkin and "Ducky" Endt (guitars) and Graham Bigelow (slide whistle).

Exhilaration may come not so much from the wind blowing against the body, spray flying in the sun, the angle of the deck challenging balance or the lunging hull beneath, as from the chance of beating the other fellow. *Spartan*, one of the famous New York Yacht Club Fifty Footers, is shown here hard on the wind in a rail-down breeze.

Power comes from a communion between the boat and those aboard. It is the feeling that together they have mastery over the elements. Straining shrouds, taut sheets and sails and driving hull seem an extension of the bodies of the crew. The will to go seems to be in the boat as well as in them. The boat is Stuart Kay's auxiliary cruising sloop *Valkyrie*.

2

2
HOW IT
ALL BEGAN

Yachting Comes to America

ONE of the first vessels built by white men in North America was a yacht. Not, to be sure, a yacht strictly in the modern sense, meaning a privately owned craft used for pleasure, but a yacht nevertheless. She was built in New Amsterdam by Adrian Block and his crew of Hollanders in 1613.

The Dutch were early yachtsmen, and the word *yacht* is derived from their term, *jaght schip*, which translates into "hunting ship" and goes along with *jaght hond* (hunting dog), *jaght peerd* (hunting horse), *jaght horen* (hunting horn), and such. In general a Dutch *jaght* was a light, fast, smallish vessel of many uses. As naval vessels they were used as dispatch boats, raiders, and for a variety of other purposes: they were revenue craft; they were state vessels used for the accommodation of high officials; they carried important communi-

cations that required prompt dispatch; and they sailed on exploring missions. The Dutch were a leading world maritime power in the seventeenth century, and some of their merchants were affluent enough to have *jaght schips* for their own pleasure; the present meaning of the word was already in use to a considerable extent among them.

Four years after Henry Hudson first sailed into the harbor of New Amsterdam, Adrian Block (the man who later discovered Block Island) was anchored in his *Tiger* at the lower end of Manhattan, just north of what is now Battery Park. Her hold was loaded with a cargo of furs bartered from the Indians, and preparations were being made for the voyage home. Alone in a strange and unsettled land, the vessel caught fire, and cargo and ship were burned beyond hope of recovery.

Fortunately the Indians were friendly, and just back of the beach, where skyscrapers now tower, there was a stand of oak ideal for shipbuilding. The rugged sailors, well used to making the most of their own resources, salvaged what little they could from the ruins of *Tiger* and set to work building a new ship. Through the fall and winter, the sour smell of oak shavings, the pungent odor of tar pots, the sound of the saw, adz and caulking iron filled the air. As the new vessel, the yacht *Onrust,* took shape, the sharp northwesterly winds that blew across the river to nip at the Dutch shipbuilders blew across the same stretch of water that 200 years later was to cradle the beginnings of American yachting.

A few years after *Onrust* sailed away, Dutch settlers were using the sheltered waters around New Amsterdam much as they did the waters of their homeland. From

The first "yacht" built in America. The *Onrust* was built on lower Manhattan by Adrian Block and his crew of Dutch sailors after their original vessel, the *Tiger,* was burned off what is now the Battery in New York, 1613. They explored the coast with her as far east as Block Island, which is still a favorite yachtsman's port of call. The original oil painting from which this photo is taken was done by Walter Bollendonk, after a careful study of available information on craft of the early 1600s to determine what her rig and hull were probably like. Leeboards, as shown amidship on the *Onrust,* are still a characteristic feature of many Dutch yachts.

the earliest days small craft were busy fishing, carrying cargo, stores, and passengers. By the 1700s, as large estates were established up the Hudson and on Long Island Sound, a few of the Dutch Patroons and the later English colonists would rig a sloop with colored curtains and a few extra con-

27

veniences. With large flags flying crisply in the breeze and leeboards trailing in the water, these first American pleasure boats were sailed beside the growing city and its outlying estates. Traditions of yachting were already established in Holland and England, but only a few were in a position to go yachting here, even to this extent.

However, many of the joys of the sport must have been known to the men who sailed the trading vessels. It is hard to imagine the skippers of two sloops, chancing to meet on a summer's day while beating down the bay to Staten Island against an afternoon southerly, who could resist the challenge to make a race of it. With the clean waters abounding in shellfish, many a crew, homeward bound after delivering a cargo, must have taken advantage of the lull caused by a failing wind to poke into a handy cove to try for a mess of oysters or scallops. Since some things hardly ever

Yachting in Colonial times. A famous old print of New York Harbor, a small section of which is reproduced here, was made in 1746, and identifies the sloop at the right as "Colonel Morris's yacht *Fancy* turning to windward." Flags seem to have run sail area a close second in those days, and arrivals and departures were marked by much firing of guns. The *Fancy* appears to be racing another sloop whose bowsprit and jib show off her lee quarter at the right edge of the picture. Col. Morris was the proprietor of a tract of land known as Morrisania, from which New York's present Morrisania Yacht Club derives its name. (Another section of this print opens Part II of the book.)

change, after a long winter, with the warm spring sun lighting a sparkling path on the water, it is easy to picture some harassed soul, with his hand on the tiller in a good slant of wind, staying on one tack longer than he really had need to, just for the fun of being alone with the wind, wave, and the good ship under him.

Although the joys of racing, cruising, and

just plain sailing were undoubtedly known to many persons who managed to grasp the time at odd moments, it was not until the 1800s that a small but active group attained sufficient leisure, wealth, interest, and skill to promise a future for American yachting. The best known of the early yachts was *Cleopatra's Barge*, built in 1816, and owned by Captain George Crowinshield of Salem, Massachusetts, one of a long line of East India merchants and ship captains. She was 83 feet of the very highest style of a luxury yacht, built at a time when there was no other such vessel available for comparison. In profile she looked like a small man-of-war, but below, the furniture was of mahogany and bird's-eye maple, with gilt bronze ornaments, and covered in red velvet and gold lace. The main cabin had imitation windows, large mirrors adorned with gilt eagles, and a chandelier. The glass and china were made specially for her, and the silver service was elaborate. On deck,

some of the rigging was woven with colored strands, and some of the lines aft were served with red velvet. She was a seaworthy craft owned by a seafaring man indulging a unique taste for luxury. She even had a

Sometimes inaccurately called "the first American yacht," *Cleopatra's Barge* was probably the first large vessel in America up to her time built specifically as a pleasure craft. An hermaphrodite brig of 83 ft. waterline and 23 ft. beam, she was built in 1816 for George Crowninshield, of the Salem merchant-ship-owning family, by Retire Becket, a builder noted for his fast merchant ships. Crowninshield died suddenly aboard the vessel in Salem harbor in 1817 after a cruise in her to the Mediterranean, and she became a cargo and packet vessel and finally wound up in Hawaii as King Kamehameha's royal yacht. The herringbone paint job shown on her port side was in many bright colors, as was a pattern of horizontal stripes on the starboard side. The cannon along the rail weren't strictly for decoration—there were still pirates in those days.

CLEOPATRA'S BARGE.

A famous yacht around old New York was the big centerboard sloop *Maria,* built in Hoboken in 1845 and said to have been modeled by Robert L. Stevens, two of whose brothers were later in the *America* syndicate. She was originally 92 feet long on the water, 26 feet 6 inches beam, and drew only 5 feet 2 inches with her seven-ton iron centerboard housed. However, she was lengthened to 110 feet and otherwise altered several times during her long life, as was customary with yachts of those days whose owners thought they had found a way to make them go faster. She raced as a trial horse against the schooner *America* in 1851, and beat her easily.

life-size wooden statue of a war-painted, feathered Indian on the foredeck.

Captain Crowinshield made one cruise in the Mediterranean with her and after his untimely death she was stripped, sold at auction, and afterwards sailed in trade. Finally, with her original intent strangely

reaffirmed, she served as the royal yacht of King Kamehameha I in the Hawaiian Islands. There she was shipwrecked.

The maritime families of Boston were not alone in their enthusiasm for yachting. The names of the Stevens brothers, John, Robert and Edwin, of Hoboken, New Jersey, are woven all through the story of yachting in the early and mid-1800s. Three of the twelve children of the early American engineer Colonel John Stevens, they each inherited their father's talent, inventiveness and scientific curiosity. They were active sportsmen, particularly interested in sailing. This interest, combined with their engineering ability, led to the development of innovations in design, rig, ballasting, and fittings that influenced all the yachting of the time. In an attempt to reduce weight aloft, they hollowed out their masts. By way of improving the efficiency of sails, they cut their sailcloth parallel to the boom (a practice which was not generally adopted until fifty years later) and attached mast tracks to the mast. To improve hull stability they moved lead ballast outside. They made experiments with multiple centerboards and even with a catamaran—a double-hulled craft inspired by the Polynesian canoes of the Pacific Ocean.

John C. Stevens is particularly associated with the New York Yacht Club, which was founded at a meeting aboard his schooner *Gimcrack* in 1844, and with the schooner *America*, which won the Hundred Guineas Cup in England in 1851, later known as the America's Cup, and still a coveted trophy in international competition. Robert L. Stevens was outstanding in railroad, steamboat, and ordnance as well as yacht design. Edwin founded Stevens Institute of Technology at Hoboken which gave the first American degree in mechanical engineering.

The New York Yacht Club, of which John C. Stevens was the first commodore—1844–1855—is generally considered the oldest American yacht club now active, although Lloyd's *Register of American Yachts* shows the Detroit Boat Club was founded in 1839 and there were a few other clubs founded before 1844, most of which were short-lived. In any case, the New York has been the dominant American yacht club for well over a century.

The span of about fifty years, from the time John C. Stevens first sailed his little craft *Diver* until his death in 1856, covered a period of dramatic change in things afloat—in merchant shipping as well as yachting. The busy harbor of New York, center of both types of sailing, was a marvelous vantage point to see the change, but the Stevens family were more than observers. They played a personal role in all of it.

At the beginning of the 1800s a big shipbuilding industry was just starting in New York. Within a few years the ships of such builders as Samuel Ackerly, Henry Eckford, Adam, Noah and Charles Brown, Christian Bergh, Jacob Westervelt, and Isaac Webb were spreading their canvas on the seas round the world. In 1800 Colonel John Stevens was experimenting with the steamboat. In 1803 he patented a propeller, and had a multi-tube, high-pressure, steam-driven boat in operation whose engine was fifty years ahead of its time. In 1808 the Stevens steamship *Phoenix* was the first American steamship to make an ocean voyage, from New York to Philadelphia. The Stevens brothers, Robert L. particularly, continued the development of steamboats, and held many patents on the steam-driven ferries that were soon plying the harbor.

In the 1820s, sailing packets, many of which were built in New York, ruled the waves. By the 1840s, steamships were setting trans-Atlantic records, and their competition as passenger and freight carriers already foretold the end of the sailing packets. The fast, hard-driven clipper ships held on through the 1850s, but the steamship, in whose origins the Stevens family had played a most important role, was at the time of John C. Stevens' death already clamorously sounding the death knell of the age of sail.

At the same time that the development of steam power brought about the end of the sailing packet and clipper ship, the Stevens brothers were instrumental in setting a trend that has brought the pleasure of sailing to more and more people. In the years before 1840, yachts were not distinctive in form, but were modeled after commercial and fishing craft. Under the experimental influence of the Stevens brothers, and exemplified in their own craft, the yacht evolved as a vessel distinctive in form and character. Though the brothers symbolize the impact of scientific inquiry on American yachting, their influence went much further. Through the vitality given the sport

The greatly increased participation and interest in yachting that followed World War II had its counterpart after the Civil War when many yachts, large and small, were built. *Fleetwing*, built in 1865, was one of the three big schooners that sailed the first trans-Atlantic yacht race, New York to England, in 1866. She lost six men when a sea swept her decks during the winter passage. George and Franklin Osgood were her owners.

by the founding of the New York Yacht Club, the wide popularity of their yacht *Maria,* and the national prominence of the *America,* they gave an impetus to the sport that lives on.

For a number of reasons, the few years around 1840 may be considered as beginning American yachting. The evolution of the hull form and rig of modern yachts can be traced back to that time, particularly to the Stevens' yachts, *Onkahya* and *Maria.* It was a period when new mathematical and scientific principles were being applied to ship design. The first course of lectures on the science of shipbuilding in this country was given in 1843 by the designer John W. Griffiths at the American Institute in New York. Specialized yacht designers such as George Steers in New York and professional designers such as Louis Winde in Boston were beginning to gain wide reputations. The program of the New York Yacht Club provided a regular schedule of regattas, stimulated an interest in racing, and provided the newspapers and magazines with a steady source of news on yachting activities.

New York and Boston were the yachting centers. With more sheltered waters and many shallow anchorages, most of the yachts around New York were shallow-draft, beamy, centerboard craft. Around Boston, the anchorages were deeper and the boats more likely to be sailed in exposed waters, so they tended to be deeper draft, keel boats. In the 1850s, on a weekend around Boston, six or seven yachts over thirty feet in length might be out sailing. By the late 1860s, about fifty of the larger yachts were centered there—an indication of the yachting boom that came at the end of the Civil War.

The first trans-Atlantic race was a part of that development, and other noncompetitive ocean crossings were made about that time, such as that of the 48-foot sloop *Alice,* under Captain Arthur C. Clark of clipper ship fame. Along shore, club races and racing cruises were regular fixtures.

While most larger yachts were manned and commanded wholly by professionals, with the owner going along to see the fun and play host to his guests and Corinthians (which is the yachting term for amateurs), on smaller boats amateurs themselves were beginning to take an active hand in the sport. The Seawanhaka Corinthian Yacht Club, for instance, was founded in 1871 specifically for the purpose of fostering amateur participation.

In smaller craft, the amateur sailor was in his element. Canoeing, particularly canoe sailing, took a great spurt in the 1860s and '70s, clubs were formed, and "canoe encampments" where the canoeists got together for a week or so each summer to discuss and compete in all branches of their favorite sport, were popular.

A picturesque phase of the sport was the sandbagger racing. The sandbaggers were smallish, flat, beamy centerboard sailing craft with enormous sail plans, to balance which they carried crews of as many men as they could get into the boats. Each man had a 50-pound sandbag which he shifted from rail to rail at each tack to keep the boat from capsizing—not always successfully. Many boats had interchangeable cat and sloop rigs, sailing in different classes on different days. Big wagers were the rule in this kind of racing, and skippers and crews were mostly "longshore characters," professionals who sometimes settled the finer points of the rules, after the race, with fists, seaboots, and empty beer mugs in some waterfront saloon. (This was certainly more colorful, although the decisions reached were probably less equitable than today's solemn protest hearings, and if it left a few black eyes, it probably cleared up grudges a lot quicker.) Sandbaggers developed around New York, spread along the coast and to inland lakes. But the rise of amateurism, and the demand for "sensible" boats, finally put an end to sandbagger racing.

At the other end of the scale in size were the sailing and paddling canoes. A noted early exponent of the type was Captain John Macgregor, retired British Army officer who built a series of canoes named *Rob Roy;* the first of them, a 15-footer of the still-popular Eskimo kayak type, in 1865. Macgregor braved the open, often-rough waters of the English Channel in his tiny craft, to the amazement of everyone.

Macgregor also cruised the canals and rivers of England, the Scandinavian countries, Germany, France, and Switzerland, and even took his canoe (designed to fit in Continental railway carriages) to Palestine and Syria. As this contemporary drawing indicates, his passage on the rivers and canals through cities and towns brought crowds of curious people (most of whom doubtless thought him harmlessly crazy) to the banks.

MORNING VISITORS.

Macgregor also had built a "big" boat, 21 feet long, yawl-rigged and of sailboat rather than canoe model, in which he cruised the British coasts extensively. In 1865 he sparked the founding of the Royal Canoe Club, and his books about his cruises are still popular reading for amateur sailors. At the time, they inspired great activity in canoeing in the United States as well as in Europe.

During the Civil War years formal yachting activities were curtailed, but six weeks after the war ended, on May 31, 1865, in the New York *Herald*, in the same edition that carried a transcript of the trial of the plotters in Lincoln's assassination, there appeared a column on summer resorts and the yachting season which began: "The war is over and everybody is prosperous." Then it went on to say:

"Yachting—the most expensive, the most healthful and the most delightful of amusements—has experienced a decided revival, and the entertainments to be given by the New York Yacht Club will fitly usher in the summer season. For four years the yachtsmen have been almost asleep, and now they are waked up and will begin to realize their dreams. New members have infused new energy and vitality into the club, and the old members are bestirring themselves with all their original vim and vigor."

Three weeks later, on June 20, 1865, under the headline "Yachting," the New York *Herald* ran a story subheaded, "A Thirty Mile Race for $1000. Play or Pay. The Great Match Race to Windward between the MAGIC and the JOSEPHINE." The story told of the race for high stakes sailed in a fog and won by *Magic*.

The revived interest in yachting and the size of the stakes raced for, must certainly have been influenced by the prosperity of the times, an interest that could not have been completely dormant even during the war. The *American Yacht List* of 1875 lists among the yachts active that season, four built in 1863, nine built in 1864, eighteen built in 1865 and twenty-four built in 1866. While the building of new yachts increased rapidly after the war, some must have been built even while the war was in progress. By the time the America's Cup races of 1870 were held the sport of yachting was flourishing.

Steam yachts were becoming popular with those who could afford them in the post-Civil War era, but they weren't regarded with complete confidence and they usually carried enough of a sailing rig to get them home in case the steam failed.

While much of the activity described here took place around Eastern centers, the sport was well established elsewhere. A yacht club at Charleston, South Carolina, and the Southern Yacht Club of New Orleans were established not much later. The sport was thriving on the Great Lakes, on some of the small inland lakes, and even on San Francisco Bay in the 1870s. Canada's Royal Canadian and Royal Halifax Yacht Clubs date back to the 1850s.

By 1880, the stage was well set for further developments in yachting.

A famous American sloop of the post Civil War era was *Fanny,* modeled and built by D. O. Richmond of Mystic, Conn., in 1874 for Charles H. Mallory. She was 78 ft. o.a., 65 ft. 4 in. waterline, 21 ft. 9 in. beam, and drew only 5 ft. 3 in. The huge single jib is characteristic of the old centerboard sloops. Extra spread to her rigging, for better support of the mast, was provided by the conspicuous channels of solid wood, so wide they were known as "Fannie's sheepwalks." This picture was taken in 1892.

A family sailing party in 1871, from *Leslie's Illustrated Newspaper*. The lady is learning to steer, under close supervision. Her flowing robes seem hardly appropriate for an active crew member on a small boat.

Enchantress, whose model (*above*), preserved in the New York Yacht Club, shows a handsome, speedy-looking hull, was modeled and built by Captain Bob Fish (*left*) in 1869. In addition to such large vessels, Fish was famed as a builder of racing catboats and sandbaggers on New York Bay for several decades, starting in the 1840s. One of his catboats, the *Una*, taken to England in 1852, set the style for a new racing class there called "Una-boats." Another, sent to Germany, perpetuated his name in that country, where all catboats became known as "Bubfisch boats." *Enchantress* herself, following the wake of *America* across the ocean (see p. 106) was raced in England. In the print below she is leading the British *Corinne* in the English Channel in 1874.

" Corinne."   " Enchantress."

THE INTERNATIONAL CHANNEL MATCH.—THE "CORINNE" AND "ENCHANTRESS" STRUCK BY A SQUALL.

A product of 1877 was the schooner *Clytie,* built by C. E. Ketcham of Stamford, Conn., for A. P. Stokes, of New York. She was 85 ft. long on deck, 78 ft. waterline, 21 ft. beam, 7 ft. 7 in. draft.

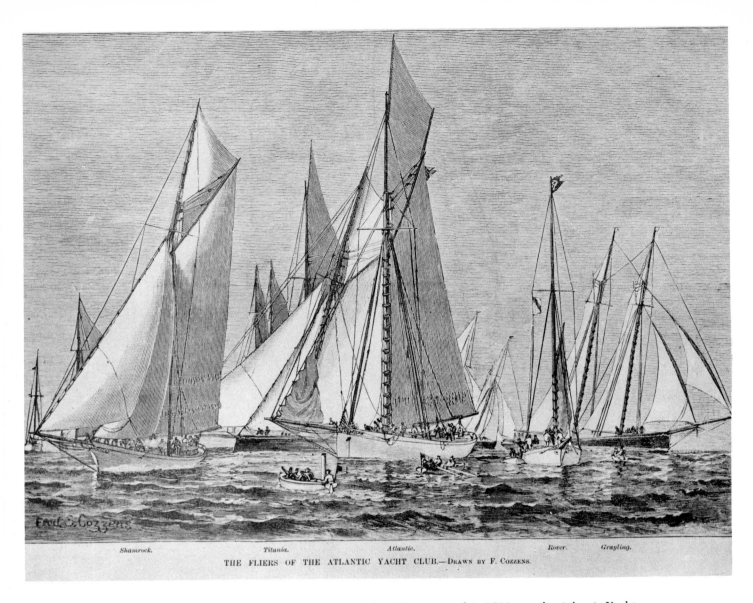

| Shamrock. | Titania. | Atlantic. | Rover. | Grayling. |

THE FLIERS OF THE ATLANTIC YACHT CLUB.—DRAWN BY F. COZZENS.

A famous yacht club organized in 1866 was the Atlantic Yacht Club, located at Sea Gate, Coney Island, New York, on the shore of Gravesend Bay. It was one of the major clubs in the New York area until commercial traffic and water pollution gradually ruined New York's Lower Bay area for sailing purposes. The club went out of commission in the middle 1930s. This Cozzens drawing shows a typical Atlantic Yacht Club fleet getting under way preparatory to a race in the 1870s.

Squalls could be just as vicious around New York waters eighty years ago as they are now. This one struck The Narrows on June 15, 1877. The schooner *Rambler* has lost her jibboom and her crew is letting the main and foresail halyards go by the run to get her lee deck out of the water. The *Wanderer's* maintopmast staysail seems to be bound for Sandy Hook. The cutter *Dora* and schooner *Active,* astern of them, have shortened sail in time to save their gear. The lads in the catboat in the foreground are bailing for their lives and even the old sidewheel tug—evidently the New York Yacht Club's official boat, from her flag—takes quite a list.

A FIVE DOLLAR SKIFF.

A SIXTEEN-DOLLAR FAMILY BOAT.

A TWELVE-DOLLAR ROW-BOAT.

A FOURTEEN-DOLLAR SAILING SKIFF COMPLETE.

The "do-it-yourself" movement is nothing new in boating. Back in 1876, for instance, *Forest and Stream,* the leading yachting, as well as hunting and fishing, periodical of its time, came out with a series of articles giving full directions, offset tables and material lists from which a man handy with hammer and saw could provide himself economically with the boat of his dreams. Starting with the $5 (material cost) skiff in which the lady seems to be trying to capsize herself into the pond lilies, they ranged through the fancier $12 rowboat, the $14 sailing skiff with spritsail, the $15 sailing canoe, $16 family boat, up to the catboat, materials for which would cost $30 in those old days of cheap lumber.

Today's "kit boat" manufacturers offer an even wider choice of products for the handy home builder to put together in his garage, but prices start at around $50 for a pram dinghy considerably smaller than that $5 skiff of 1876.

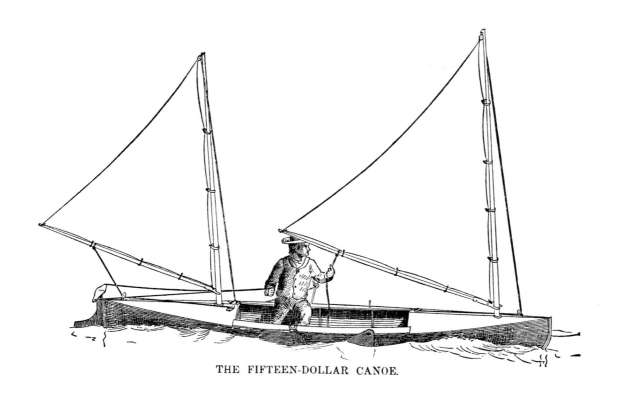

THE FIFTEEN-DOLLAR CANOE.

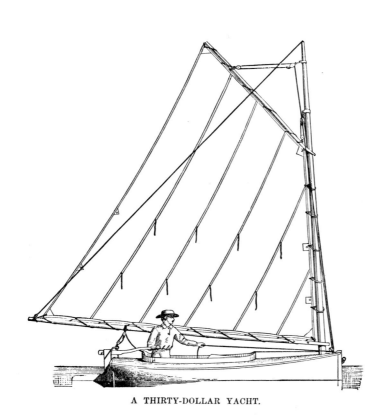

A THIRTY-DOLLAR YACHT.

Few yachtsmen now alive remember the heyday of the sand-baggers, which was about over when this picture was taken of the *E. Z. Sloat* in 1896. These broad, shoal centerboard hulls carried enormous rigs, and were kept from capsizing (usually) by their big crews and the 50-pound sandbags they shifted from rail to rail at every tack. An old sandbagger, the *Annie*, is preserved in Mystic Seaport by the Marine Historical Society of Mystic, Conn.

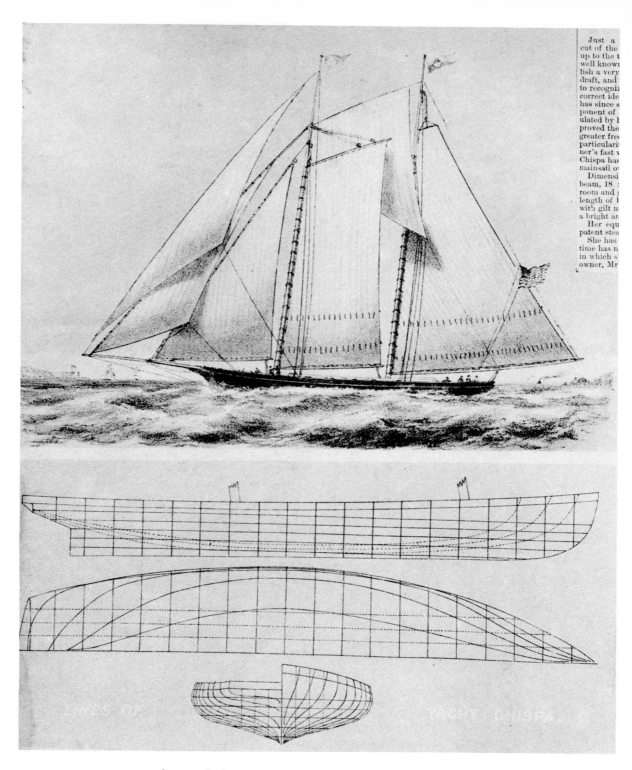

The East had no monopoly on yachting even as far back as 1879, when Matt
Turner built the schooner yacht *Chipsa* on San Francisco Bay. Her lines
show a very beamy, shoal-draft, centerboard hull of great stability well
suited to carry sail in the prevailing strong winds on the shallow waters of
the San Francisco Bay area. The almost triangular mainsail is interesting in
view of the fact that the jib-headed rig didn't become popular in most areas
until the 1920s. But this type of sail was used on the Block Island fishing
boats of *Chipsa's* time, and comes down from the Dutch through several
centuries. In the normal 25-mile-or-better Golden Gate afternoon breeze,
you don't want too much sail aloft.

Innovation and Change

TODAY, when racing is done either in one-design craft or in yachts built to measurement rules which cause them to conform, within reasonable limits, to certain standards, it is difficult to realize the variations in yacht design of the 1880s. In those days, every yacht was an individual creation, reflecting the effect of local or national types and uses; the personal beliefs of her designer and builder, and the idiosyncracies of her owner. There was less standardization, and more of a chance that a designer would come up with something that would make his new boat outstandingly faster—or regrettably slower—than her rivals.

By 1880, the yachting population was embroiled in the famous cutter-vs.-sloop controversy which produced arguments running into millions of words—some of them pretty hard words, too—in the public press and round the yacht club bars.

New York was the center of yachting activity, and racing here was done for the most part in protected waters. There were many shallow spots which a boat of deep draft would have to skirt, but which a shoaler boat could cut across. Due to this, the popular type of craft became the very shallow draft centerboard "skimming dish." This was true even of very large yachts, as many home moorings were in shallow harbors. They were boats of very high ratio of breadth to length, which gave them the power to carry big sail plans in fresh breezes—up to a certain point. If the skipper carried his sail too long in the face of rising winds, or got caught unprepared in a sudden squall, his boat might be driven beyond her limit of stability and capsize—with none of today's lead ballast keels to bring her back up again.

The extreme example of this New York

Bay type was the schooner *Mohawk*, built in 1875 for Commodore William T. Garner. On an over-all length of 140 feet and waterline of 126 feet, she had a beam of over 30 feet and drew only six feet of water. She had a huge sail plan, 235 feet from the bowsprit end to the tip of her main boom, and 163 feet high to her main truck. Experts who viewed the skimming-dish type with alarm predicted that she'd drown somebody. Their chance to say "I told you so" came one July afternoon when a sudden squall caught *Mohawk* with almost all sail set, just ready to drop her mooring at Stapleton, Staten Island. Over she went, and six persons, including the owner's wife, were carried down with her and drowned.

Here were new arguments for the proponents of safe and scientific yacht design.

Meanwhile, some American yachtsmen

New Bedford, Mass., has been a yachting center since the organization of its yacht club in 1877. This harbor scene of that port in 1883, with a typical whaling bark providing local atmosphere in the background, shows the schooner yacht *Ruth*, built at Noank, Conn., in 1881; *Metric*, a fast small cruising sloop of the time; and at the extreme right a Roslyn sharpie.

had visited England and seen an equally extreme but opposite type—the British cutter, which was narrow and deep. If the New York centerboarder looked like a plank lying flat on the water, the extreme cutters justified the nickname of "planks on edge" that was applied to them. They heeled very easily in light breezes, but heavy lead ballast either stowed inside or bolted to the bottoms of their keels prevented their going all the way over. If hatches and skylights were tight, you could lay one of these craft

flat on the water, and when the wind eased she'd come up again. There were differences in rig, too—cutters usually had housing bowsprits and topmasts that were lower and run inboard in heavy weather, and they carried double head rigs (jib and forestaysail) while the centerboarders usually had fixed spars and single big jibs.

Robert Center, Roosevelt Schuyler, C. Smith Lee, and William P. Stevens formed the hard core of what became known as the "cutter cranks." Mr. Stephens, who carried the torch for this group in the press through his *Forest and Stream* yachting columns, still liked to refer to himself, at ninety-odd in the 1940s, as "the last of the cutter

In the 1880s the "cutter cranks," admirers of the narrow, deep British type of yacht, were feuding, afloat and in print, with the adherents of the beamy, shoal-draft New York Bay type sloops and schooners. *Bedouin* was an American-built cutter of 1883, designed by John Harvey and built by Piepgrass for Archibald Rogers of New York, a leading "cutter crank." Her dimensions are given as 83 ft. 10 in. over all, 70 ft. waterline, 15 ft. 8 in. beam, 11 ft. 6 in. draft, and she carried 5,196 feet of sail. For her time and type, *Bedouin* was a conservative design with more than typical cutter proportions of beam to draft. In some extreme cutters, the draft was equal to or even greater than the very narrow beam.

The profile and mid-section of *Clara,* an extreme cutter with a draft greater than her narrow beam. Designed by Will Fife, Jr., in 1884, she was brought to the United States in 1885 by Charles Sweet, a London lawyer temporarily residing in New York. For the next few years she had an outstanding racing career, beating all competition, including a new compromise cutter and a new sloop built just to defeat her. Her success was hailed by the "cutter cranks." *Clara* was 63 ft. 9 in. over all, 52 ft. 9 in. on the waterline, 9 ft. beam and 9 ft. 8 in. draft. With only nine foot beam, she was almost six times as long on the waterline as she was wide and had actually eight inches more draft than beam.

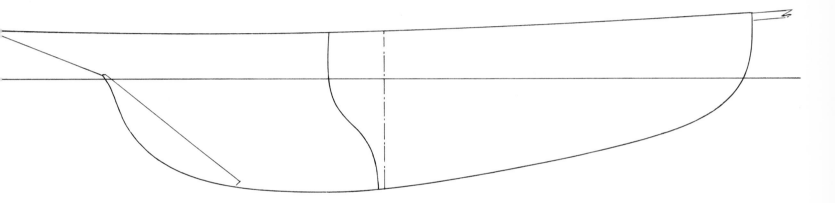

cranks." The designers naturally took sides, too, the older rule-of-thumb modelers and builders generally sticking with the traditional American type, the more scientific architects such as A. Cary Smith plumping for the cutter type. Some cutters were built here, and a few British cutters were brought over, and made converts by their good performance in most conditions.

As typical examples of the two types, here are the dimensions of two yachts that raced in New York Bay in 1881. The British-built cutter *Madge* was 46 feet on deck, 38 feet, 4 inches waterline, only 7 feet, 9 inches beam, and drew 7 feet, 5 inches of water. The sloop *Wave,* 41½ feet on deck, 38 feet waterline, was 14 feet in the beam and drew

only four feet. *Madge* raced on New York Bay in 1881 against *Wave* and several other good boats of her type, and won consistently. Cutter stock went up.

Proponents of the two types went at it hot and heavy, in the press and verbally, for years. But as might have been expected, the ultimate answer lay between the two extremes. The cutters had their bad points, too—so narrow that there was no comfort in them, so tender that they always sailed at a sharp angle of heel. A compromise type evolved: wider than the cutter and not as deep; deeper of body than the sloops, less beamy, and with ballast stowed deep in the hull, or bolted on the keel. The better features of the two rigs were also merged.

A handsome example of the centerboard sloop yacht of her day was *Eclipse*, modeled and built in 1881 by Epinetus Willis of Port Washington, L.I. She was 54 feet long on deck, 49 ft. waterline, 17 ft. beam and 4 ft. 3 in. draft. She had a double head rig, i. e., forestaysail and jib instead of the huge single jib of the older centerboard sloops. This adoption of the double head rig—far easier to handle—probably reflected the cutter influence. *Eclipse* was the largest yacht built by "Neet" Willis, famous for his sandbaggers and other fast smaller craft.

The profile and mid-section of the centerboard sloop *Arrow*, designed and built by David Kirby of Rye, New York, in 1874. Typical of the large racing sloops of her time, she was one of the fastest in her class. Her dimensions were: 66 ft. 8 in. long, over all, 61 ft. 3 in. on the waterline, 20 ft. 2 in. beam and 5 ft. 6 in. draft. With a beam of more than twenty feet, she was just over three times as long on the waterline as she was wide, and had almost four times as much beam as draft.

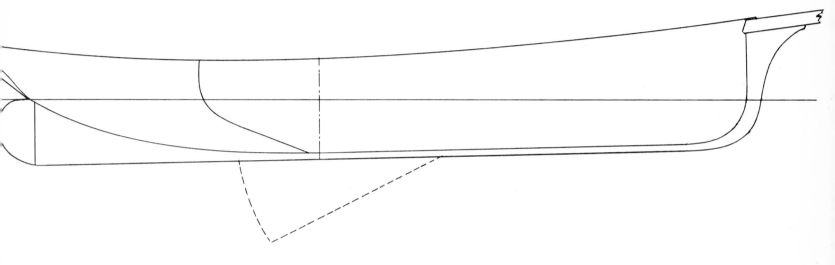

Fine examples of the conservative model were the America's Cup defenders *Puritan, Mayflower,* and *Volunteer* of 1885–87, designed by Edward Burgess of Boston—where they never did think much of either the New York or the British freaks, anyhow.

So things settled down on a pretty sensible basis, and there was some fine racing and a good deal of yacht design development, along in the later 1880s, in classes like the 40-foot waterline boats in which all the leading designers of the day, and many of the leading racing skippers, took part. Then along came another departure in yacht design that in a few years had changed the whole appearance of the yachting fleet.

The year 1891 marked a revolution in yacht design, born in the fertile brain of Nathanael G. Herreshoff, "the Wizard of Bristol," whose reign as America's greatest yacht designer and builder was just starting. Hitherto yachts had had either plumb stems or graceful, concave "clipper" bows. When a new 46-foot waterline racing class was organized, to be rated by a "length and sail area" measurement rule, Herreshoff built for E. D. Morgan a sloop, *Gloriana,* whose most conspicuous feature was a long, overhanging bow, and whose performance consistently left her conventional rivals fighting for second place away back in her wake.

Actually, what "Mr. Nat" did was to cut

away the forefoot of the hull of conventional design, giving it a blunt, round entrance compared to the sharp, often hollow, bow waterlines then in vogue. It had several beneficial effects. By shortening the waterline, it permitted more sail to be carried for a fixed rating. It reduced wetted surface, making less frictional drag and thus improving light-weather speed. It gave a long actual sailing length when heeled down so that much of the overhanging bow and counter sides were in the water, providing the stability and power to carry a big rig in strong winds.

Within a year or two every yacht designer was trying to copy the *Gloriana* bow in his new racing boats, and the bows of many existing boats were cut off and rebuilt in long overhangs. As usual, the new technique was overdone. Racing and even many cruising yachts came out with long, flat overhanging ends which were structurally weak and made them miserable things when slamming and banging to windward in rough water. Such ends, carried to extremes, are seen today on a few special types, like the Inland Lakes scows, designed to sail in smooth water, or at least no worse than a short chop.

Eventually owners, designers and rule-makers saw the mistake of overdoing this principle for all-round use. It was brought under control by new rating formulae such as the Universal, International and (much later) Cruising Club Rules, under which favorable ratings are attained with ends that are sea-kindly and structurally strong as well as speedy.

Racing developed rapidly in really small, as well as in larger yachts toward the end of the nineteenth century. One impetus was the presentation of the Seawanhaka Cup.

The Seawanhaka Cup—officially entitled the Seawanhaka Corinthian Yacht Club International Challenge Cup—is sometimes described as being to small craft racing what the America's Cup is to big yachts. It

Merchant ship captains trading to the Orient early in the 19th century had brought home wondrous tales of the speed and stability of the double-hulled canoes, or catamarans, used by the South Sea Islanders, and the type was well known here by 1880. Nat Herreshoff and his brother John had brought one to New York and given the racing fleet there such a beating that the "cats" were promptly ruled ineligible to race against respectable yachts. But these "proa ladronias," pictured on Cayuga Lake, N.Y., in 1880, were obviously designed not for racing but for leisurely sailing of the "park lake" variety. Modern catamarans have made ocean passages, and under their ideal conditions of fresh reaching breezes make some amazing speeds—their adherents are still trying to make them acceptable as ocean race contestants.

one for Norway. Currently, Canada holds it by virtue of a victory in the 1956 match.

The early races were in boats around 15 feet on the waterline, known as "half-raters." In 1922, after twelve years of no activity for the cup, it was put up for the Six-Meter Class, then new in this country, and has been raced for in those boats ever since, except for one match in Eight-Meters.

While most of the foregoing is on yacht racing, let's not overlook the fact that the companion sport of cruising was growing rapidly, too. More and more people were finding the enjoyment of getting away in sailing craft, small boats that one or two men could handle readily. There were rare adventurers who shoved off across oceans in small and often unsuitable craft, but most cruising was done along the coast with only an occasional night at sea. Such areas as Maine and the Chesapeake were already favorites of the East Coast cruisers; San Francisco Bay and the Puget Sound area had much to offer on the West Coast; Great Lakes cruisers were discovering Mackinac Island, the North Channel, and other good cruising grounds, and a few hardy pioneers like Commodore Ralph Munroe had braved the wilderness and opened up southern Florida as a spot to sail in.

What was to become a boon to the cruiser —simon-pure windjammers may cry "No, No!" if they like—was just beginning to make itself heard (and smelled)—the gasoline-driven internal combustion engine. They were rackety, undependable contraptions in those days and few sailormen would deign to have one of the nasty things in their fine, clean sailboats. But the gas engine had come to stay, and to improve. The vogue of the pyrotechnic naphtha launch had come and was going out by 1900. But for motive power other than sail, steam—coal-fired—was the standard in big luxury yachts, high-speed "commuters" and small launches when the nineteenth century ended.

has never attracted as much attention from the public at large as has the latter, but it has gotten around a lot more. Put up by the club for which it is named, it was first raced for in 1895 at Oyster Bay, New York. Since then there have been thirty matches for it.

Successfully defended the first time by *Ethelwynn,* designed by W. P. Stephens, it was soon captured by the Canadians, thanks largely to the genius of G. Herrick Duggan, an engineer who designed bridges for a living and designed and sailed small boats for fun. It stayed in Canada through nine matches, came to Massachusetts Bay for two more, and subsequently has been won intermittently by the Scotch, the Norwegians, and the Americans. The score runs twelve wins for the United States, ten for Canada, seven for Scotland, and

By 1883 steam yachts like *Stranger* and *Atalanta,* shown here
steaming up the Hudson River along the Palisades, were
more dependable than those of earlier times, but they still
carried sails bent to the spars, "just in case." The steam launch
Rover (foreground) and the old Hudson River cargo sloop were
typical contemporaries.

East of Cape Cod, neither the extreme deep, narrow cutter nor the flat centerboard skimming-dish found favor. The more conservative yachtsmen of New England favored a practical, seaworthy type of racing and cruising yacht, midway between the extremes in beam, draft, and displacement (weight), with either single or double head rig. Such are *Lillie* and *Ella May*, shown here sailing near Boston in 1884.

This one was entitled "Still the champion, with a few moments to spare." Can the lady in the over-sized hat, and her pug dog, be a racing crew? Rigs of the old-time catboats look enormous for the size of the hulls, by contrast with today's smaller but more efficient sail plans.

Unlike the big-yacht owners who were content to sit back and let their professional crews do it all, small-boat sailors were never a sedentary lot. The small-craft racing man has to be something of an acrobat as well as a sailor. The spring meet of the Hudson River Canoe Club gave the canoe sailors a chance to show how spry they could be. This is from a *Harper's Weekly* of the 1870s.

Iroquois, 98-ft. over all schooner, was designed by
A. Cary Smith and built by Harlan and Hollings-
worth, who turned out many big steel yachts, in
1886.

Probably the keenest and most competitive racing class of the later 1880s and early 1890s was the 40-foot waterline class. Built to a rule which permitted wide variations of other factors, while holding waterline length to 40 feet, this class attracted both owners and designers. The leading architects of the day all turned out 40-footers, experimenting with all combinations of beam, draft, hull form, sail area, weight and other factors. Edward Burgess, of America's Cup defender fame, was one of the leading designers in this class. Typical of his Forties was *Choctaw*, built in 1889, 39 ft. 9 in. on the water and 53 ft. over all.

Katrina, one of the great 70-ft. waterline class sloops, was designed by A. Cary Smith and built by Piepgrass at City Island, N.Y., in 1888. Described as a "compromise cutter or sloop," she had a centerboard, was steel-built, and measured 93 ft. 3 in. on deck, 21 ft. 6 in. beam, 9 ft. 3 in. draft. In this picture her crew are shifting topsails, setting one before hauling the other down. *Katrina* survived for 40-odd years and, rerigged as a schooner, was flagship of the Larchmont Yacht Club, under Commodore James B. Ford, in the 1920s.

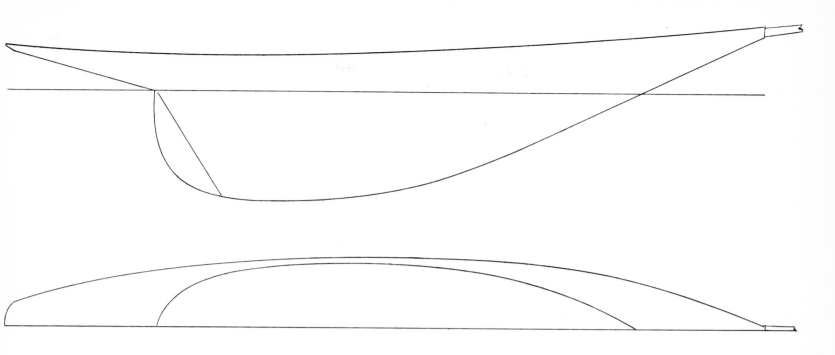

Profile of *Gloriana*.

Detail of forefoot of *Gloriana*. The shaded area shows the outline of a conventional bow prior to 1891, cut away by Herreshoff in the design of *Gloriana*.

The craft that revolutionized sailing yacht design in the 1890s was the 46-foot Class sloop *Gloriana*, designed and built by Nat Herreshoff in 1891. Her most conspicuous feature was that where until then yachts had either been plumb- or clipper-bowed (i.e., with vertical or concave stems) Herreshoff gave *Gloriana* a long forward overhang, which as she heeled down made additional length on the water, with resultant increased potential speed and sail carrying power. Other features were cutting away of the forefoot (i.e., the "knuckle" under water where the stem came down and met the keel); less displacement (weight) than most of her class; and more rounded form at the forward end of the waterline. She also embodied revolutionary Herreshoff ideas in light construction and in rigging details. *Gloriana* won practically every race she sailed in her first year, and there was a great scramble among other designers to copy her features; especially the *Gloriana* bow.

65

A handsome example of the great steam yachts of the latter part of the 19th century—the "millionaires' floating palaces" in the popular parlance of the day—was *Narada*. Built and engined in Scotland, as were many of her American-owned type contemporaries, she was 224 ft. over all, 194 ft. waterline, 27 ft. 2 in. beam, 14 ft. draft. Her accommodations fully merited that word "palatial," and were designed for luxurious living for the owner and a small number of guests, in contrast to today's practice of cramming the maximum possible number of berths into the smallest hull that will hold them. Another marked contrast to today's high horsepower in small cruisers—*Narada's* triple-expansion steam engine had a "nominal horsepower," by Lloyd's standards, of 127 hp. Her speed was in the neighborhood of an honest 14 knots. The sails she carried were mainly for decoration. She was a well-known yacht for many years under the ownership of Henry Walters, of Baltimore, Md.

New and old in the mid-'90s. After Herreshoff brought out *Gloriana* with her revolutionary overhanging bow in 1890, others lost no time in copying it, and the shape of a racing yacht's bow was the tip-off to her age. In this picture the plumb-stemmed *Eclipse*, built by Epinetus Willis in 1881, and the "spoon-bowed" *Eidolon*, designed by Charles Olmsted in 1894, show the difference.

For the ultimate in speed and thrills under sail, wait until the water gets hard. Speeds of well over 100 miles an hour are claimed for iceboats, under the right conditions. These iceboaters were sailing on the Hudson River back in the 1880s, but judging by the fleet of cargo sloops under sail in the background the main river channel must have been open water. And if this boat doesn't catch her runner in that crack in the ice, smash herself up, and send her crew flying out in a bruising and possibly wet spill, they'll be lucky.

Typical of many moderate-size steam yachts used for coastwise cruising was *Aquilo*, owned by William P. Eno, of New York. Designed by Tams, Lemoine and Crane and built by Lawley in 1901, she was 152 ft. over all, 125 ft. waterline, 12 ft. 5 in. beam, 9 ft. 4 in. draft, and was driven by one triple expansion engine.

Yachtsmen who were around Larchmont and
Rye, N.Y., in the 1930s remember *Audax* as a
quaint survivor of a vanishing type of cruising
yawl. She was designed by John Hyslop for John
P. Clarke and built in Fall River, Mass., in 1893,
and was still going strong 40 years later. She was
43 ft. over all, 30 ft. waterline length, had a deep
keel.

Ohysis was a typical smart cruising sloop of the Gay Nineties. Smart, too, were the long-skirted, sailor-hatted, necktied costumes of the ladies aboard.

facing page above:
A development of the 1880s and 1890s was the very fast—though neither seaworthy nor handsome—scow-type sailing craft, which have since been brought to a high state of development in the Inland Lakes. *Oogrook*, shown here, was one of the early scows.

facing page below:
By the later 1880s, sailing canoes had evolved into highly developed racing machines. The old standing lug sails were replaced by sliding gunter rigs, with the leaches of the sails extended by full-length battens. And Paul Butler, a diminutive cripple, had invented the sliding seat, to enable him to get his light weight out beyond the rail for leverage.

below—The Seawanhaka Corinthian Yacht Club International Challenge Trophy, put up in 1895 by the club of that name at Oyster Bay, L. I., has been to small yachts more or less what the America's Cup has to big ones. It was first competed for in "half-raters" of about 15 feet waterline. Its first winner, representing Seawanhaka, was *Ethelwynn*, designed and sailed by William P. Stevens—a yachtsman whose career as a sailor, designer, writer and historian spanned three-quarters of a century beginning in the 1870s. That he was ahead of his time is attested by *Ethelwynn's* triangular mainsail, shown here 25 years before the jib-headed rig was generally accepted for racing. The trophy has been won 12 times by American yachts, 10 times by Canada, seven by Scotland and once by Norway, and in recent years has been raced for mostly in Six Meter Class sloops.

Square-rigged yachts, like these two brigantines (hermaphrodite brigs, technically speaking), were not very common even back in 1900. The black one is *Aloha,* built in 1899 for Arthur Curtiss James from designs by Tams, Lemoine and Crane. For the benefit of those who may wonder, the sails on her foremast, starting with the lowest,

were called foresail (clewed up in this picture), fore lower topsail, fore upper topsail, fore topgallantsail, and fore royal. Headsails, from inboard out, are forestaysail, jib, flying jib, and jibtopsail. Three main staysails, mainsail and maintopsail complete the rig. Mr. James later had another

Aloha, bark-rigged, i.e., three masts, square-rigged on the fore and mainmasts and fore-and-aft rigged on the mizzen. *Lady Godiva*, like the clipper ships of an older day, carries studdingsail booms rigged on her mainyard. She was British-owned.

Toward A National Pastime

A FLEET of Yachts made a very different picture in 1900 from the one that it had presented twenty years earlier. The distinctive national types of racing yachts, such as the British cutter and the New York centerboard sloop, had merged into almost a common type which was different from either of its predecessors—light displacement, long-ended, fin-keel racing machines. Extreme examples of the type were the America's Cup defenders and challengers of 1901 and 1903, and, in the smaller-boat field, the Sonderklasse sloops, 30-odd feet long, in which American yachtsmen did some generally unsuccessful racing against German and Spanish rivals around 1907.

Not that there weren't plenty of old-type

By 1900, a new type of large racing yacht had been evolved which looked little like those of a decade before. Long ends, rather shoal hull sections and deep, lead-ballasted fin keels characterized most of the new racing classes. Such a group was the New York Yacht Club 70-foot waterline one-design class, three of which are shown here getting away to an even start on a beat to windward. Their dimensions were 106 ft. over all, 70 ft. waterline, 19 ft. 5 in. beam and 15 ft. draft. Four of them were built by Herreshoff in 1900; *Rainbow* for Cornelius Vanderbilt, *Mineola II* for August Belmont, *Virginia* for W. K. Vanderbilt and *Yankee* for H. B. Duryea and H. P. Whitney.

yachts in commission—some handsome clipper bows graced the scene down through the 1930s—but when you saw a plumb or a clipper stem, you knew that she was a boat past her racing prime or that she was a cruising boat whose owner hadn't "gone modern" and followed the fad for the new racing-type lines.

As a matter of fact, the extreme "fin keel scow" type didn't stay in favor long. Although fast, they proved bad sea boats, hard on men and gear, unfit for rough-water work offshore, and so fragile of construction compared to the stresses and strains set up in them that they racked themselves to pieces in a few years of racing. There was a demand for a new measurement rule that would produce healthier, abler, more durable yachts.

With such a demand established, it wasn't long before the rules came. The Universal Rule—largely the work of Nat Herreshoff and the New York Yacht Club— and the International Rule of the International Yacht Racing Union, which took in most of the European yachting countries, were both in force by about 1908 and better boats were being built to their standards. There were minor differences in the types they produced: the R, Q, M, J and other classes here; the Meter classes abroad. The

One of the Seventies, Cornelius Vanderbilt's *Rainbow,* making knots to windward in a rail-down breeze. Sail plans were not unlike those of big yachts of the '90s, in that they carried gaff mainsails, topsails, staysails, jibs, and flying jibs as working canvas. But note that, where most of the older yachts had sails up-and-down cut (i.e., with the cloths running parallel to the leech, or after edge) most new racing sails were made with the cloths at right angles to the leech. Better sailcloth, preferably Egyptian cotton, and improved sailmaking technique were required to make these sails hold together and keep their shape, but they were faster than the old up-and-down-cut sails, just as today's sails of Dacron and other synthetics outpull cotton sails.

American rule still tended to produce a slightly wider boat than the International— but only slightly. Basically the two types were not far apart. The International may not have been a better rule, but its Six, Eight, Ten and Twelve-Meter sloops were being brought to or built in this country in the 1920s and early '30s. From that time on, few yachts were built to our Universal Rule, though some are still sailing under it. The 1937 America's Cup boats, *Ranger* and *Endeavour II*, were about the last built to the Universal Rule, and the contenders for that historic trophy in 1958 will be Twelve-Meter sloops built to the International Rule.

Another development that had barely started before 1900 but gained rapid headway after that date was the swing to one-design racing classes. Having a boat built exactly like that of your racing rivals was an unthinkable thing a few decades ago. Pride of ship was the heart of the sport. If your friendly enemy was regularly showing you his yacht's transom in the races, you and your naval architect got your heads together and decided what kind of a new boat would turn the tables. You sold the old boat to someone who wanted her for cruising, or perhaps somebody who raced in a less keenly competitive area; or maybe even —perish the thought—to someone who felt he could get more speed out of her than you'd been getting.

This got to be an expensive business, as boat-building costs followed the eternal pattern of inflation. There are some very definite advantages to one-design classes. For one thing, the more identical boats you build, the lower will be the per-boat cost, due to manufacturing savings. For another thing, now that racing is practically a 100 per cent amateur sport, an owner is out to prove that he's a better sailor than his rivals. This is more clearly subject to definite proof—or disproof—if your boats are all exactly alike, at least to start with. A third point is that one-design classes, when they reach the numbers and distribution some of them have today, lend themselves to intersection and international racing. You can go to a series thousands of miles away without the expense of taking your own boat, step into a chartered or borrowed boat there, and be almost as much at home as in your own.

So the trend to one-design classes has become strong. Of course the bigger the boats, the fewer the owners. Only three yachtsmen had the means and inclination to build sloops to the New York Yacht Club's 70-foot waterline class in 1900. When the 50- and 40-footers were built a few years later, there were eight or nine Fifties and a few more Forties. But when you get into the small classes, there are several in the 16–25-foot length range in which the numbers now run up into several thousand. As an example, take the history of the Stars, oldest of these big-numbered classes and the one which set the pattern on which several others have been organized and operated.

Back in 1909, a class of 17-foot, one-design, fin-keel, chine-built sloops was active on Manhasset Bay, Long Island. George A. Corry and other owners got the notion that such a boat, but a bit larger, would make a fine "poor man's" one-design class that might stimulate interclub competition.

An enlarged Bug, called the Star, 22 feet, 9 inches long, 5 feet, 8 inches beam, 3 feet, 4 inches draft, was designed by William Gardner and in 1911 Ike Smith, of Port Washington, Long Island, built the first twenty-two of them, for $260 a boat. It caught on not only for interclub but for interstate, international, and intercontinental racing. Corry and George W. Elder guided the Stars' destinies for some forty years, and did it so well that the class now numbers nearly 4,000 boats, spread among 37 countries. The first Star International Championship was held in 1923 and since then, while most of the world champions

America's Cup trial race in 1901. *Constitution* (foreground), built that year was expected to beat the 1899 defender, *Columbia,* but the latter, with Charlie Barr in command, won the trials and became the only yacht ever to defend the Cup twice.

Nepsi and *Winsome,* of 1907, break out their
jibs and square away for the starting line.

have been Americans, others have hailed
from Germany, the Bahamas, Italy, and
Cuba.

Changes in rig and other details to keep
the class up to date, so that it would con-
tinue to appeal to keen racing skippers,
have been adopted from time to time, but
the older boats, if well maintained and
modernized, can still compete with the new
ones. But old Ike Smith probably spins in
his grave nowadays when someone pays
ten times as much for a Star with "all the
fixin's" as he charged for the first boats.

Another gradual change in the picture
of the racing fleets during the first two decades of this century was in the sail plans.
The gaff rig was still almost universal, but
it went up in the air and pinched in at the
bottom. Engineering on masts and rigging
helped make this possible, and even before
the aeronautical industry came along with
its wind-tunnel tests, designers and yachtsmen realized that there was more wind up
high, and perhaps even that a sail with a
tall leading edge had more drive going to
windward.

So rigs became taller and narrower. The
long bowsprits that used to shove sailors
right through the next approaching sea,
and the long booms that hung a rod or two
out over the sterns, were gradually shortened up. Eventually the bowsprits disap-
peared altogether and the booms were
chopped off just over the taffrail. Single jibs
came back into style, but tall, narrow jibs,
not the broad triangles of the old-style
sloops. Mainsails went farther up taller
masts, and gaffs were peaked up at a sharper
angle, except in the bigger boats where a
topsail was to be set over them.

It was after World War I that aircraft
engineering began to be applied to sail
design, and tall, triangular, "Marconi"
mainsails began to come into general use.

The steam yacht continued to be the
rich man's luxury in the larger sizes, for
diesel engines didn't come into use in pleasure craft until after World War I. The
gasoline motor, however, caused the real
revolution in boating between 1900 and
1920. Motors rapidly improved: less noise
and vibration; less dirt thrown around the
boat; more power per pound of iron; and
most important of all, more dependability.
They didn't break down very often, and
when they did, on-board repairs were usually within the competence of the average
citizen, who was learning something about
engines in automobiles, too.

It was a long, uphill fight before the gasoline auxiliary engine could be established
in most sailors' minds as a respectable ad-
junct to the cruising sailboat. But it was
noticeable that almost nobody who put
one in ever took it out, except to get a better
one. It was simply too handy in those calm
spells, and extended the range of your
cruises and the general utility of your boat.

Some sailors turned to out-and-out motorboats, but the big push was among men who
had never learned to sail but who figured
that a motorboat was something they could
understand and operate. So a whole horde
of newcomers took to the water for their
pleasure, once the gasoline engine was developed beyond its first uncertain stages.
They have been coming ever since, until
today the Coast Guard believes there are
some five or six million pleasure craft in
use—most of them motorboats.

To the sailor of sail, this needn't be dis-
couraging. The number of sailors has skyrocketed too, and some of the men who
went afloat first in motorboats have now
taken to sailing. The two branches of sport
afloat are spreading fast and supplementing each other.

The gasoline-driven "speedboats" of the early 1900s were of the type exemplified by *Peter Pan Jr.* whose speed, evidently, wasn't enough to blow those big straw hats off her fair passengers. The boats were of round-bottom model, extremely narrow, with jacknife-sharp bows.

above:

In the first decade of the 20th century it was a much-argued question whether the newfangled gasoline-engine-driven "auto-boats" would ever equal the fast steam-driven yachts in speed. The world's motorboat speed record in 1907 was under 35 m.p.h.; the steam yacht *Arrow* had made 45 m.p.h. One of the fastest of the steamers, shown here, was Howard Gould's *Niagara IV,* built in 1903 by Consolidated at Morris Heights from Charles L. Seabury's designs. With an over-all length of 111 ft. and waterline of 104 ft., she had only 12 ft. 3 in. beam and drew only 4 ft. 3 in. of water. Twin triple-expansion steam engines drove her.

below:

Around 1910, the hydroplane, a speedboat very different in hull form than the *Peter Pan, Jr.,* was introduced. The hydroplane at speed lifted and skipped along the surface of the water rather than plowed through it, and speeds began to soar toward the present record of over 220 miles per hour.

A start of the K Class off Eaton's Neck, L.I., in 1907. The boats are *Istalena,* George M. Pynchon; *Winsome,* Henry F. Lippitt, and *Aurora,* Cornelius Vanderbilt, the latter carrying a club topsail while the other two have working gaff topsails set. The boats, sister ships built by Herreshoff in 1907, were 85 ft. 2 in. over all, 62 ft. 8 in. waterline, 16 ft. 7 in. beam, 10 ft. 10 in. draft.

Aurora, her spinnaker set, approaches the windward mark.

Two of the famous schooners of the first decade of this century were *Ingomar* (left) and *Elmina*, owned respectively by Morton F. Plant and Frederick F. Brewster. Both schooners were 87 ft. waterline, and about 126 ft. on deck. Here they have just completed a tack. *Elmina's* boomless "lug" foresail isn't fully sheeted home yet, *Ingomar* hasn't quite filled away, and both fore-topsails are still clewed up, as they had to be when these schooners tacked, to clear the main-topmast and spring stays. Note the masthead man on the foremast spreader aboard *Elmina* (*detail above*).

facing page above:
The *Bug*, forerunner of the Star Class sloop, with George Corry at the helm and Mrs. Corry crewing.

facing page below:
One of the first Star races, in 1911. The original rig was called a sliding gunter—a compromise between gaff and triangular sail. The leader here is *Little Dipper* (No. 17), sailed by George and Mrs. Corry.

below:
A recent Star race. The rigs and general appearance of the boats have changed a good deal, but note that an old boat, No. 202, Adrian Iselin's *Ace*, kept up to date with all the improvements, is right in there with the much newer—as the sail numbers show—Stars.

What the well-dressed commodore will wear! Cornelius Vanderbilt was commodore of the New York Yacht Club in 1906–1908 and, standing on his quarter-deck, he really looks the part—choker collar, long-glass and all. He was also, like several others of his family, a real sailor, as he proved in *Rainbow*, *Aurora*, and other racing yachts.

Commodore Cornelius Vanderbilt's flagship was the steam yacht *North Star*, a fine example of her type and time. Designed and built in England in 1893, she was 256 ft. over all, 219 ft. 6 in. waterline, 29 ft. 2 in. beam and 16 ft. 6 in. draft. Her single triple-expansion steam engine had, according to Lloyds, 223 nominal horsepower.

It took a lot of men to run a steam yacht properly. These 42 officers and men, including 11 in the steward's department, manned the steam yacht *Cassandra*, 284 feet long, built in Scotland in 1908 for Roy A. Rainey.

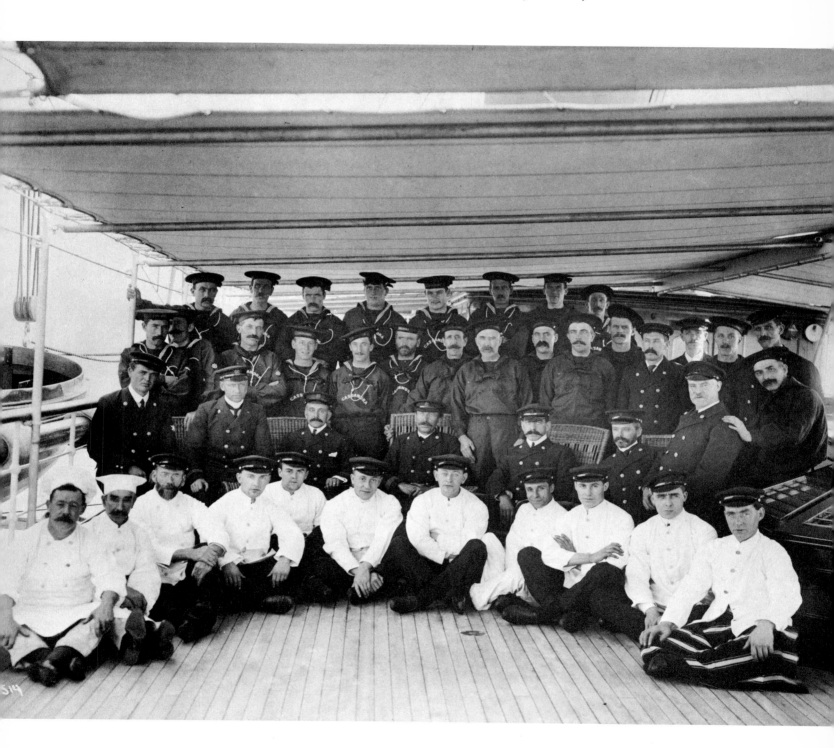

For every big steam yacht like *North Star* and *Cassandra* there were hundreds of small power cruisers and open boats up and down the coast. This scene of about 1908 is the landing of the Columbia Yacht Club, located on the Hudson River shore of Manhattan. An old club, founded in 1867, the Columbia battled with New York Harbor's increasing dirt and traffic until the 1930s, then moved to Long Island Sound.

One of the New York Yacht Club's great classes was the Fifties. This is the start of one of their first races in 1913, the year they came out of the Herreshoff shops. They were 72 ft. over all, 50 ft. waterline, 14 ft. 6 in. beam, 9 ft. 9 in. draft. Some of them are still sailing and one, J. V. Santry's *Pleione*, now schooner-rigged, has won major trophies in the past few seasons.

Another great class was the Fighting Forties, built by Herreshoff in 1916 and later. Like the Fifties, they were owned and sailed by some of the sport's best skippers. Husky, able ships, some of them were rerigged for ocean racing, and did very well at it, too. But there's such a thing as too much wind, even for a Forty. *Chinook* would probably be going faster without that big topsail to heel her lee deck under. The Forties are 59 ft. over all, 40 ft. waterline, 14 ft. 5 in. beam, 8 ft. draft, and were originally gaff-headed knockabout (i.e., without bowsprit) sloops, as were the Fifties.

The masthead men of the old, gaff-rigged big sloops and schooners—the steeplejacks of yacht racing—had plenty to do aloft, keeping the gear in shape and the sails setting right. The coming of the jib-headed rig, with no topsails, spelled the end of their permanent stations aloft. *Resolute (facing page)* was the last of the America's Cup defenders that carried regular mastheaders while racing, in 1920.

However, there comes a time on every racing yacht when somebody has to shin up aloft and fix whatever has gone wrong, as in this International one-design class sloop.

3

3

THE

AMERICA'S CUP

The Pattern of Victory

NO trophy in yachting has ever been sought with more persistent effort, more lavish expenditure of money and skill, or more intense public interest, than the old silver jug known as the America's Cup. Captured in England by a Yankee schooner in 1851, it has been defended by the New York Yacht Club against fifteen all-out attempts to win it back by yachtsmen from various parts of the British Empire.

Many millions, both in dollars and pounds, have been expended on the cup matches, and on occasions bitter controversies over the races have fallen only slightly short of becoming diplomatic crises. Yachts built to race for the cup have exemplified the finest in design, construction, rigging, and equipment, and they have often made advances in these areas that were ulti-

mately to improve yachts of all classes and sizes.

The quest is still on. As this book is published, the New York Yacht Club is preparing to defend against another British challenger, which comes from the Royal Yacht Squadron, the same club from which the *America* took her cup in 1851.

The first race set the tone of international rivalry that characterizes the cup matches. It was planned at a time when British national pride ran high as England prepared to play host to the Great Exhibition, the first World's Fair of 1851. Organized by Prince Albert, the fair was planned as an exhibition of the scientific and industrial progress of the age. Captains of industry were found-

This model of the *America*, now in the model room of the New York Yacht Club, shows the sharp, concave bow lines that characterized her and some of Steers' contemporary pilot schooners, a contrast to the "cod's head and mackerel tail" hull form of most yachts and other small vessels of her time. Note also the simplicity of sail plan and rigging.

ing great fortunes ashore and captains of the hard-driven clipper ships were seeking new records afloat.

American sailing clipper ships, famed from the Spice Islands to the Baltic for their speed, dominated the ocean trade routes of the world. Almost as outstanding, though less widely known, were the pilot schooners of New York and other American ports, which went far offshore in all weathers, racing to put their pilots aboard inbound vessels. Yachting, however, had only recently become an organized sport in America. The New York Yacht Club had been founded in 1844, and while its fleet ranged from New York Bay "skimming dishes" to seagoing schooners, it included a number of vessels modeled after, or actually converted from, pilot schooners. Nowhere did the United States feel more pride in her achievements than in the speed of her sailing ships. Therefore when a British merchant suggested that an American yacht participate in the races to be held during the summer, there was immediate response. American industrial exhibits might suffer in comparison with the British but perhaps an American yacht could compete in earnest.

Commodore John C. Stevens and Mr. George L. Schuyler of the New York Yacht Club decided to show the world what a fine pilot-boat-yacht looked like and how she could sail. Less altruistically, they hoped to put the project in the black by winning from the British some of the big cash stakes and bets that were customary in yacht racing in those days.

A syndicate of Club members was formed, and then commissioned George Steers, a young modeler and builder of outstanding pilot schooners, to design and build their yacht. After the usual delays, which have traditionally beset the building of new yachts, they took delivery of the *America* on June 18, 1851, and paid Steers $20,000 (about the price of a good 35-foot cruising sloop in 1956).

The *America* was a typical New York pilot boat, though below, the mahogany sofas were covered with velvet and the decorations were Chinese white and gold. She was 101 feet, 9 inches long over all, 90 foot, 3 inch waterline, 23 foot extreme beam and 11 foot draft. She carried 5,263 feet of sail in a working rig that was amazingly simple compared to the rigs carried by later schooners—mainsail, foresail, and one big jib. The sails were of cotton duck, well cut, and more effective as motive power than the somewhat baggy flax sails carried by British yachts of the day. In referring to their cut the London *Times* was later to call them "flat boards." Her form, too, was a departure from the traditional cod's-head-and-mackerel-tail shape of most yachts here and abroad—with sharp, concave bow lines, her greatest beam aft of midships, and fairly powerful sections aft.

She was sailed across to France by a professional crew headed by Sandy Hook pilot Dick Brown, since few owners braved the rigors of an offshore yacht passage in those days. At Havre she refitted, Commodore Stevens joined her, and she sailed across the Channel to Cowes. On the way, a fast British cutter, *Laverock*, came out to meet the stranger. Cannier men might have pulled a few punches, but Stevens and Brown sailed the *America* all-out. She beat *Laverock* so badly that, when the news spread, no British yachtsman would agree to meet the Yankee schooner in a match for the kind of stakes that Commodore Stevens and his fellow owners had in mind.

On reaching Cowes, Commodore Stevens sent a note to the Earl of Wilton, Commodore of the Royal Yacht Squadron, which, in effect, challenged all yachts of England to a race. Lord Wilton replied with the suggestion that the *America* enter a race open to vessels of all rigs and nations for a new cup of 100 guineas value. Commodore Stevens, still looking for a match race, replied with the following note:

My Lord—

Although it would be most agreeable to me that this race should be run for a cup of limited value, yet if it is preferred, I am willing to stake upon the issue any sum not to exceed 10,000 guineas. I have the honor to be your Lordship's obedient servant,

J. C. Stevens

The English press chided the Royal Yacht Squadron for its embarrassing lack of enthusiasm to meet the contender, but the *America* could find no challenger. The summer was one of inactivity, with the exception of a chance meeting on August 15, after which the papers reported that *America* sailed right through the fleet of forty vessels she met in East Channel during a Royal Victoria Yacht Club regatta.

Finally, on August 22, *America* was one of fifteen yachts in the race for the Royal Yacht Squadron cup around the Isle of Wight. The starting gun found the yachts moored in a double line off the harbor at Cowes, where the race was to begin and end. At first the winds were light and variable, and *America* sailed in the midst of the fleet; but after an hour the wind freshened and came from ahead, a condition very favorable to *America*, since she was able to sail much closer to the wind than the British yachts. Soon she was leading the fleet, there to stay until the finish. Had the wind stayed light and variable over a course affected by changing tides, the race might have gone to the yacht with the most luck; but under the circumstances the result was decisive enough for the English to hail an American victory.

Tradition has it that when *America* crossed the finish line in the gathering twilight, an old quartermaster aboard the royal yacht answered Queen Victoria's question of which boat was second with: "There is no second, Your Majesty." It seems unlikely that this really occurred, however, since the smaller cutter *Aurora* finished only seven minutes after *America*.

The London *Times* proclaimed the *America's* victory "the triumph of the year," and stated, "We have been beaten, signally defeated on our own element, our Yacht Squadron routed." Chagrin was not the only note struck in the British press. They drew attention to the *America's* design, and to her sails and rigging. The race which had grown out of the scientific interest in the first World's Fair ended with the London *Times* urging British yachtsmen to adopt

John C. Stevens, first commodore of the New York Yacht Club from its founding in 1844 to 1855, headed the syndicate that had the *America* built in 1851. He joined her in France after her trans-Atlantic passage, and managed her campaign in British waters. He was a leading engineer as well as a sportsman, and was a member of the family that founded the Stevens Institute of Technology in Hoboken, N.J. The other members of the syndicate were his brother, Edwin A. Stevens, George L. Schuyler, Col. James A. Hamilton, J. Beekman Finley, and Hamilton Wilkes. In 1857 Commodore Stevens and the other owners deeded the Hundred Guineas Cup, which had become known as the America's Cup, to the New York Yacht Club as a perpetual challenge trophy for international match racing.

the new scientific theories of hull and sail form whose efficiency the American designers had demonstrated. Within the next three years it is said that over one hundred English yachts were altered or built with the long hollow bow that had helped the *America* distinguish herself in international racing.

Commodore Stevens and his associates sold the *America* to an Englishman and came home with the Hundred Guineas Cup to show for their efforts. The *America* subsequently enjoyed a checkered career: British yacht; Confederate blockade runner; sunk in the St. John's River, Florida; taken, raised, and used as a Union Navy dispatch boat; Annapolis midshipman training ship; American-owned yacht again. She was finally purchased by a group of yachtsmen who presented her to the United States Naval Academy in 1921. In 1945, too far gone with decay to be kept afloat, she was broken up at Annapolis.

Back home the trophy, which in New York had come to be called the America's Cup, graced Commodore Stevens' drawing room until 1857, when he and his co-owners deeded it to the New York Yacht Club, under terms which specified that any organized yacht club of any foreign country should always be entitled to challenge for it in a match race.

The first challenge came from James Ashbury of the Royal Thames Yacht Club and the race was held in 1870. The early correspondence between Mr. Ashbury and the New York Yacht Club was hardly marked by friendly compromise. Mr. Ashbury originally proposed a contest against a single American yacht, to be settled in three races around Long Island. Neither this nor later proposals brought "mutual consent" and the New York Yacht Club finally decided that the conditions of the race were to be similar to the first race at Cowes—a single race against the fleet.

Mr. Ashbury's *Cambria* was a fine, seago-

THE CLIPPER YACHT "AMERICA".

The *America's* flat-cut, machine-woven, cotton sails, clearly shown in this print by Currier and Ives, were credited with much of her superior speed over the British yachts with their loose, hand-woven flax canvas. The four other schooners shown are *Capricorn, Gypsy Queen, Karita* and *Surprise*, the three former, rivals in the Isle of Wight race.

THE GREAT INTERNATIONAL YACHT RACE, AUGUST 8, 1870.
FROM THE CLUB HOUSE, STATEN ISLAND AROUND THE S W SPIT TO AND AROUND THE LIGHT SHIP AND BACK 40 MILES
For the Queen's Cup won by the AMERICA at Cowes, in 1851.

The first race for the America's Cup, on New York Bay, August 8, 1870. *Magic* and *Idler* are leading; then comes *America,* rerigged since 1851 and looking tiny in this company. *Dauntless* is fourth here and *Cambria* fifth. *Cambria* had to sail against twenty-three American schooners and sloops in this event.

Sappho winning the last 1871 race against *Livonia.* The three spectator steamers seem to be "blocking" for the defender—they're certainly doing the challenger, astern of them, no good. From *Aquatic Monthly and Nautical Review,* 1872.

The Sappho rounding S. W. Spit in her last race with the Livonia.

ing schooner. She beat James Gordon Bennett's schooner *Dauntless* in a race across the Atlantic on her way here. But she was no match for a fleet of twenty-three sail, including some fast, light yachts of local bay racing types, over the New York Yacht Club's own bay course.

The spectator fleet was large, enthusiastic and noisy. Steamboat whistles, booming guns, brass bands and shouts of encouragement apparently added excitement to a race which itself provided little. *Magic,* a light centerboard schooner, went quickly to the lead and won easily. *Cambria* was the eighth yacht to round the lightship and finished tenth. The old *America,* with a Navy crew from Annapolis, was fourth.

Painstaking care had gone into the preparation of *Magic* for this race. Ballast had been shifted, tried, and shifted again, to get the most speed out of the hull. Sails had been tried, recut, altered again and again for maximum performance. The crew had been drilled until each man was expert in his job. As a result *Magic* went to the starting line, a vessel in top form with a crew completely capable of taking advantage of every break. When the gun went off, *Magic* was the first craft to weigh anchor, come about and trim sails on the first leg of the course with a show of smart maneuverability that impressed all of the spectator fleet. This combination of a well-tuned craft and an expert crew has consistently brought rewards throughout the history of racing for the cup.

That year Mr. Ashbury sailed *Cambria* in the New York Yacht Club cruise and in a series of match races afterwards, but *Cambria* was a slower craft than her American competition and Mr. Ashbury built the schooner *Livonia* for a new challenge in 1871.

The conditions agreed upon for the new challenge were somewhat different. The races were to be between two yachts, the winner to take four races out of a possible

seven. However, the defending yacht could be selected for each race from a group of four yachts to be named. The four defending yachts selected were *Columbia, Palmer, Dauntless,* and *Sappho.* The last two had sailed across the Atlantic and were known as fast heavy-weather keel yachts, while *Columbia* and *Palmer* were fast light-weather centerboard yachts. With the defending club having the choice of a fast light-weather yacht or heavy-weather yacht for each race, the advantage was on its side. The race might be in the spirit of "friendly competition," but the Cup obviously was not being given away.

The results of the contest might have been anticipated. *Columbia* won the first and second races, and lost the third. *Sappho*

Galatea (above), the challenger, and *Mayflower,* defender, of the 1886 America's Cup match. The two yachts look much alike in these photos, with their long bowsprits, plumb stems, and long counters. Their rigs, though differing in mechanical details, are quite similar, with big club topsails, jib topsails, jibs and staysails. But in design each represented her national type of the era. *Galatea* was the narrow and deep (15 feet beam, 13 feet 6 inches draft) British cutter, while *Mayflower* was the typical American sloop of ample beam (23 feet) and moderate draft (9 feet 9 inches) with her centerboard up, though she drew 20 feet with the board down.

won the fourth and fifth to retain the Cup. There was probably more fight before and after the races about the terms and results of the contest than there was during the series. The turmoil, however, did help lead to more favorable rules for succeeding challengers.

The third challenge came in 1876 from Canada when the yacht *Countess of Dufferin* arrived to meet the defender *Madeline*. Sufficient funds to outfit and tune up the challenger were not available, and in the contest she was hopelessly outclassed by the defender. This situation occurred again four years later in 1881 when a new Canadian challenger *Atalanta* met *Mischief*.

The fifth challenge, in 1885 from Sir Richard Sutton of the Royal Yacht Squadron in England, was of particular interest to yachtsmen here. It introduced a competition between Boston and New York yachtsmen for the chance to defend the Cup, a rivalry that continued through the years. It also brought to a boil the controversy between the sloop men and "cutter cranks."

As yachts of different size raced each other, it rapidly became evident that a good big craft was faster than a good small one, and various systems of time allowance were devised. At first these systems were by tonnage, then by some variation or combination of length, breadth, depth, or sail area. Whatever the system, it strongly influenced the form of racing craft, as a yacht

Yacht designing genius of the 1880s was Edward Burgess, of Boston, who produced, among other outstanding craft, the America's Cup defenders *Puritan* (1885), *Mayflower* (1886), and *Volunteer* (1887). The first was financed by a Boston syndicate headed by General Charles J. Paine, who privately owned the other two. Burgess died at the age of forty-three in 1891, just before the reign of Nat Herreshoff as the Cup boat designer, but his genius survived in his son, W. Starling Burgess, designer of the three defenders of the 1930s, *Enterprise*, *Rainbow* and *Ranger*.

built to race is built by a man who wants to win, and the rules are studied to be used to the best advantage.

In America up to 1883, there were five general rules governing time allowance, and despite the rule adopted in 1859 when a trend toward deeper, narrower yachts could have occurred, American yachts generally remained broad, shallow centerboard craft.

In England, the rules early penalized beam, and the cutter developed slowly into a narrow, deep keel craft growing narrower and deeper as lead ballast was used outside.

In 1881 the cutter *Madge* was shipped over from Glasgow, and in a series of match races with typical American sloops, handily won six out of seven starts. The success of *Madge* raised serious doubts about the relative ability of contemporary British and American yachts. The yachting press was filled with the debate, the advocates of either form sometimes going to extremes in their opinions. A third group involved believed basically in the sloop, but felt that some of the features of the cutter could be incorporated into the sloop design to advantage, in a compromise form.

When Sir Richard Sutton's *Genesta* challenged in 1885, there were no American sloops large enough to be successfully matched against her, and James Gordon Bennett, Commodore of the New York Yacht Club, and William P. Douglas, Vice Commodore, announced they would build a new defender. The news that a Boston group, headed by General Charles J. Paine, was going to build a yacht designed by Edward Burgess of Boston was treated as something of a joke by the New York papers. Burgess, who had studied to be a naturalist before turning to yacht design, was not well known, while the designer for the New York Yacht Club syndicate, A. Cary Smith, was outstanding.

Puritan, the new Boston yacht, was a compromise design, with less beam and deep draft, and with a heavy outside lead keel and a large centerboard. In this change from a traditional form to a newer design, the New England product proved superior to the one from New York. In the trial races, *Puritan* showed she was faster than *Priscilla*, the New York Yacht Club sloop, and she was chosen to defend the cup.

The race between *Genesta* and *Puritan* was to go to the winner of two out of three starts. One race to be held on an inside course in Lower New York Bay, the other, or others, to be sailed in the ocean off Sandy Hook. The contest was held in September when good racing weather might be expected, but as so often happened during these events, the winds proved contrary, and the first two attempts at a start were called off for lack of wind.

On the third try, *Puritan* fouled *Genesta* during maneuvers before the start and was disqualified. Though *Genesta* might have sailed over the course alone to score a win, her owner declined to do so. The first actual race was sailed over the inside course in light airs, and *Puritan* won easily. The next race, sailed at sea for the last twenty miles in a stiff wind, was also won by *Puritan*, this time in a close, hard-fought match.

In 1886 the English challenged again, the new cutter *Galatea* five feet longer than the previous challenger, but otherwise similar. The new defender, *Mayflower*, designed by Burgess for General Paine, was a little larger than but similar to *Puritan*. The races were held in light airs, and *Mayflower* far outsailed *Galatea* to retain the Cup to the delight of the nation, and most particularly of Boston.

Though the American yachts were "compromise sloops," there was considerable difference between the hulls of the English and American yachts in these two contests. *Puritan* and *Genesta* both were 81 feet long on the waterline, but *Genesta* was 15 feet in beam and *Puritan* 22 feet, 7 inches in

A spectator fleet watches *Volunteer*, with her spinnaker set, come rolling home well ahead of the hope of Scotland, *Thistle*, in 1887.

beam, and *Genesta* was 13 feet, 6 inches in draft and *Puritan* 8 feet, 8 inches. The English cutter had one-third less beam, and was over one-third deeper in the water. In ratio of length to beam, *Puritan* was three and three-fifths as long as she was wide, and *Genesta* was five and two-fifths as long on the waterline as she was wide.

One result of the defeat of the English cutters in these races led to a change in the rule of rating in England that had produced their narrow cutters, and in future contests, the yachts of the two countries tended to be more alike in dimensions.

After the races of 1886 the Royal Clyde Yacht Club offered to challenge, and ex-pressed a willingness to enter into negotiations earlier than the seven-month period before the actual race, a period established in the Deed of Gift of the Cup. This was thought to be of advantage to the defending club in their preparations to meet the challenge, but the offer was turned down with some hard feelings incurred. These were aggravated when the new challenger, *Thistle*, arrived and on being measured before the race was found to be over a foot longer than the length previously announced. Burgess had designed the new defender *Volunteer* for General Paine, his third design in three years to defend the cup.

Thistle, built under the new British rule of rating, was beamier than the previous two challengers. On the same waterline length she was over five feet wider. In an effort to cut down surface friction, the designer had so cut down the underwater surface that insufficient lateral plane was left, and though she sailed as fast through the water as *Volunteer,* she could not hold up as well in going to windward. The results were the same as the previous two races, the American craft winning easily.

These last three contests marked the end of an era insofar as one yachting aspect of the craft was concerned. Burgess, referring to *Puritan,* wrote, "The object in building *Puritan* was not so much to get a vessel that would be particularly fast in light weather as to produce a good all-round yacht, and especially one that would give a good account of herself in a breeze of wind." These craft had been "good all-round yachts," capable of cruising as well as racing. The owner and his party, as well as the crew of *Genesta,* slept and ate on board during the races, just as they would if they were cruising. From 1887 on, contestants for the Cup had nominal or no living quarters aboard. Tenders moored in the harbor, or accommodations ashore provided for the crew. The yachts became the most scientifically advanced racing machines their designers and builders could produce.

Lord Dunraven of the Royal Yacht Squadron brought over the next challenger in 1893. The Deed of Gift of the Cup had been changed after the last contest with the new rules providing new difficulties for a challenger, and correspondence went on for several years before a satisfactory mutual understanding was reached. The new series was to go to the winner of three out of five races, all sailed at sea on an outside course. Instead of full details of the hull dimensions of the challenger to be provided ten months before the race, which would have frozen that design long before the race, only the

waterline length was required at that time.

Three new American yachts were built to meet the challenge, and a fourth was building when it was received. Burgess, after a short but very active and successful career as a yacht designer, had died of typhoid fever in 1891. Nathanael G. Herreshoff, who became a legendary figure in the field of yacht design, succeeded Burgess as the designer of Cup defenders. His design *Vigilant* was chosen to meet Lord Dunraven's *Valkyrie II,* and retained the Cup by winning three straight races.

Two years later Lord Dunraven was back with a new *Valkyrie III.* In his writing, Lord Dunraven showed a keen understanding and sensitivity to many aspects of yachting and yacht design. His personality seems to have been contradictory, however, and in 1895 his impact on the international yachting scene was explosive.

In an excellent article on the problems of a yacht designer in contending with the diverse elements involved in design, he wrote, "A sailing ship is a bundle of compromises, and the cleverest constructor is he who, out of a mass of hostile parts, succeeds in creating the most harmonious whole." The contest in 1895, however resulted in more disharmony, hostility, and ill feeling than has ever been generated in any international yachting event.

Even the trial races between *Vigilant* and the new Herreshoff design, *Defender,* had their heated moments. On two occasions Captain Charles Barr of *Vigilant* gave way to *Defender* during close maneuvering to avoid the chance of a collision, though both times he felt he had the right of way and was being taken advantage of. By the time *Defender* was selected to meet the challenger the trial races had provided more than their usual excitement and controversy. By September, general interest in the race ran high. On the morning of the start the New York *Times* reported that on the day before, when both craft were in

Clipper bows came back into fashion in 1887 with *Volunteer* (*above*) and *Thistle* (*on facing page*). Again, while they appear quite similar in rigs, the hulls followed national characteristics which, however, were not as far apart as before. *Thistle* was relatively broader than her British predecessors; *Volunteer* was a bit deeper of hull than older American boats. On approximately 85 feet waterline, *Thistle* had 20 feet 4 inches beam and 13 feet draft; *Volunteer* 23 feet 2 inches beam and 10 feet draft.

118

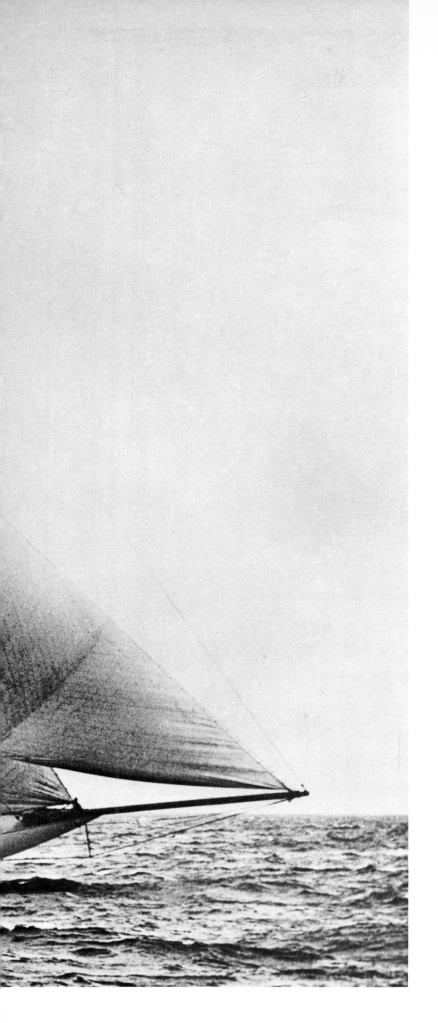

drydock at Erie Basin for last-minute over-haul, at one time in the afternoon over 8,000 persons were present in the yard to look at the contenders, and about 20,000 persons had visited the yard during the day.

Dozens of steamers were available to carry passengers to the race course. The accommodations were varied. The Old Dominion Line Steamship *Yorktown* could carry 500 passengers at $5 per head, the *City of Lowell,* 800 passengers at $3, the charge on the *General Slocum* was $2. Fifteen thousand persons sailed out to see the great yacht race.

The crowding of the spectator fleet was a nuisance at the starting line. The first race came after a three-day easterly blow and the sea was rough. *Valkyrie III* had been designed for the wind and water conditions which usually prevailed off Sandy Hook in September. She was three feet wider than *Defender,* and the lumpy sea and light wind was not to her liking. *Defender* won by over seven minutes, and though a shift in the wind might have helped her in the first half of the race, she outsailed *Valkyrie* on the way to the finish, and the race seemed to indicate she was the faster boat.

After the race the yachts were taken to Erie Basin and remeasured after Lord Dunraven indicated to the committee that *Defender* was lower in the water than her measured waterline. When questioned by a reporter, Mr. Watson, designer of *Valkyrie III* who was aboard during the races, said, "The difference from the first

First of the Cup defenders designed and built by the great Nathanael B. Herreshoff was *Vigilant,* which defeated Lord Dunraven's *Valkyrie II* in 1893. These sloops, with their long overhanging bows and fin keels, marked a drastic change in hull form since 1887, and there was little difference between national types. Here *Vigilant,* with working headsails and a small gaff topsail set over her single-reefed mainsail, is walking up to windward in a strong breeze.

All hands on the main halyards as the huge main-sail slowly goes up. The bearded skipper is the famous Hank Haff; most of his crew were Down-Easters from Deer Isle, Maine. This deck scene is aboard *Defender*, which defeated Lord Dunraven's *Valkyrie III* in 1895. The series that year ended in protests and much hard feeling.

measurement was very slight and would change the time allowance very little." The New York *Times* stated that as a result of the new measurement, "The *Defender's* waterline was made one inch less, and the *Valkyrie's* a quarter of an inch more."

The second race set the scene for a grand fiasco. Again the spectator fleet crowded the starting line. As the two yachts approached the line the steamer *Yorktown* interfered with their course. Just short of the starting line *Valkyrie* was to windward, *Defender* just to leeward of her, and the committee boat to windward and ahead of both of them. Suddenly *Valkyrie* seemed to put up her helm and fall off toward *Defender*, then luffed up sharply and turned away. As she did so the end of her boom passed over *Defender's* windward rail and snapped her

starboard topmast shroud. *Defender's* top-mast bent like a bow, but held. The incident occurred right under the committee boat. Both vessels went over the starting line, were not recalled by the committee, and went on to finish the race. *Defender* sent men aloft, made some repairs and, despite being at a serious disadvantage, made a close race of it, *Valkyrie* winning by less than a minute.

Defender protested. After a hearing

Valkyrie III was disqualified, and the race awarded to *Defender*. Before the protest was acted upon, Lord Dunraven sent a letter to the Cup Committee requesting that because of the crowding by the spectator fleet the next race be postponed and a clearer course selected.

His request was not met to his satisfaction. At the start of the next race the spectator fleet was out in force, but held off at a respectful distance. The two yachts started, but immediately after the start, *Valkyrie III* hauled down her racing pennant and retired from the course. *Defender* went on alone to score a win and retain the Cup.

The papers were filled with a bitter controversy. Some members of the Race Committee had appeared of divided opinion in regard to the disqualification. Lord Dunraven said his action had nothing to do with the protest but was a result only of the crowded conditions of the course. He had suffered an unfortunate experience in this respect the year before on the Clyde when *Valkyrie II* was rammed and sunk by the *Satanita* just before the start of a race. A steam yacht on the course had been involved in the incident so this interference had a special meaning to him.

Whatever Lord Dunraven's justification for his actions, the issue was confused and many people were heatedly partisan about it. In retrospect it seemed to all an unfortunate conclusion to an event that was becoming symbolic of good sportsmanship. That the two yachts should have come into contact when maneuvering sharply in such close quarters was not so improbable as it may seem. *Valkyrie's* main boom was 105 feet long. In turning, the outboard end swung in a wide arc, well outside the stern and far wide of the man at the wheel. The slightest misjudgment could be serious. It was unfortunate that all the complex contributing factors to the incident should have combined to produce such a disharmonious conclusion.

It is a tribute to the inherent good sportsmanship in yachting that the next challenge from Sir Thomas Lipton, which started under a cloud of suspicion as to his motives in contesting, should have ended by setting a new tradition of good sportsmanship under difficult and trying conditions.

Valkyrie III was the center of bitter controversy.

The second Herreshoff Cup sloop, *Defender,*
spread a lot of sail with spinnaker and balloon
jib supplementing her mainsail and club topsail.
Here, she needs a pull on the spinnaker sheet.
Note the cameraman in the stake boat under the
Defender's bowsprit in the above detail. The
cumbersome tripod-mounted cameras of the
period used 8-by-10-inch glass plates.

124

Defender in drydock. She was typical of the racing machines of her era, with a light displacement hull and a deep fin keel. Her construction was unusually light, with bronze plating below the waterline and aluminum topsides, and she was broken up after a few years when electrolysis began to eat out her plates.

The Lipton Challengers

THE internationally troubled waters stirred up by the Dunraven controversies were calmed by Sir Thomas Lipton, representative of British efforts to regain the America's Cup from 1899 to 1930.

Sir Thomas was a colorful figure. As a poor boy in Glasgow he started as a grocery clerk, amassed a chain of stores, and became a dominant figure in the merchandising of food in the British Isles. He owned a large steam yacht, *Erin*, but before his challenge for the Cup he had shown little interest in sailing.

Despite the suspicions of the British press that Lipton's real interest in the races might be in their attendant publicity, he was received warmly in the United States. His personal charm, gallantry, and graciousness in defeat soon won him the lasting affection of the American public. Sir Thomas was a wonderful source of copy to newsmen and cartoonists. One of the incidents that made him well known to millions of readers occurred when he rushed off in his launch during a squall, to aid in the rescue of some yachtsmen in distress.

Lipton first challenged in 1899, with the

129-foot sloop *Shamrock* designed by Fife of Fairlie. *Shamrock* was a racing machine, designed and built for the course and the race, with no expense spared. She was meant for only one purpose: winning the Cup. Unfortunately for Sir Thomas, however, the Americans also excelled at this game. In Nat Herreshoff, designer and builder of the new defender *Columbia*, there was a fortunate combination of designing ability and great mechanical ingenuity. Such yachtsmen as J. Pierpont Morgan, who commissioned the building of *Columbia*, provided the interested wealth to build the best and to offer competition for testing the new craft in trial races. C. Oliver Iselin, manager of *Columbia*, was one of a number of men with long experience in racing and tuning up these largest of racing cutters. Captain Charles Barr, her sailing master, and the greatest professional racing skipper ever to handle a wheel, had command of a highly skilled crew. The combination of talent in design, finance, management, and seamanship was formidable; not only could it build a good, fast yacht, but it could run her at maximum performance.

The innovations of the "Lipton races" were not confined to the yachts themselves. There was a new method in the coverage of the first Lipton challenge which kept public interest at a high pitch. The New York *Herald* and the *Evening Telegram* had made arrangements with Marconi to report the race from the course on his new wireless

The hard feelings of the Dunraven era were soon cured by the sportsmanship and personal popularity of the next challenger, Sir Thomas Lipton, Irish baronet and chain store magnate who was to be five-time loser between 1899 and 1930, with his succession of *Shamrocks*. The first of them is shown here on the wind with Sir Thomas's steam yacht *Erin* standing by.

telegraph. On Sunday, October 1, 1899, the New York *Herald* ran a headline which told of "Complete details of the marvellous invention by which news is reported forty miles away without the use of wires."

The story began: "Absolute demonstration of the value of the Marconi system of wireless telegraphy will be furnished to the western world for the first time during the yacht race this week by Signor Marconi and a corps of assistants who will report every movement of the contending yachts to the Herald. This will be a feat unparalleled in the history of journalism."

Each day news of the yachts was flashed to shore and the wonder of this new invention kept interest high despite delays caused by defects in *Shamrock's* rigging and by calm, dreary weather. When a race was finally sailed to a finish, Marconi's wireless sped the word of *Columbia's* victory to shore long before any other means of communication. Visibility was limited to four miles, and the *Herald* was pleased to report that the "mist baffled land observers, and signal balloons and carrier pigeons alike failed."

Marconi's final story, flashed from the course, told of another successful defense of the Cup. In the second race *Shamrock* lost her topmast and withdrew. *Columbia* proved the faster and better handled of the two yachts and won the match in three straight races. Captain Barr's smallest winning margin was over six and a half minutes for the 30-mile course.

Lipton went home happy despite his defeat. He had proved himself a good sportsman, and he was showman enough to enjoy the crowds that swarmed to the course afloat, and clustered around the bulletin boards ashore, as much as they enjoyed him. He tried again in 1901, 1903, 1920, and 1930.

Sir Thomas said that the first *Shamrock* had cost between $400,000 and $500,000, exclusive of the outlays of bringing her across the Atlantic and providing for tenders, maintenance, and crew while here. In succeeding years, as the costs of materials and services rose, this expense increased. In recent times, with the expense running into millions of dollars, there is a dual challenge in maneuvering these ultimate of racing machines to the starting line. The challenge of costs must be overcome before the challenge on the course can be met.

Herreshoff's *Columbia* was the only yacht to defend the America's Cup twice. Under the flawless handling of Captain Barr, she beat the new Herreshoff *Constitution* in the trials. The contest between *Shamrock II* and *Columbia* in 1901 was a close one, and Lipton was back in 1903 with new hopes. This time the defender, *Reliance*, beat *Shamrock III* by an easy margin.

Reliance, which defended against *Shamrock III* in 1903, was the ultimate development of the "fin keel scow" type of extreme racing machine, with long, flat overhangs, a shoal, beamy hull and a deep, lead-loaded fin keel. She was 143 feet, 8 inches long over all, 89 feet, 8 inches waterline, 25 feet, 8 inches beam, and 20 feet draft, and lugged an enormous rig of 16,160 feet of sail. Her main boom was 108 feet long. *Shamrock III*, carrying some 2,000 feet less, was dismasted in one of her early trials, but Herreshoff's engineering produced a rig and spars that successfully carried *Reliance's* "acres of canvas" except on one occasion, when her topmast broke in a trial race. *Reliance* won the first race by 7 minutes, 3 seconds, the second by 1 minute, 19 seconds, and *Shamrock III* did not finish the last race, being badly off her course in a fog.

The huge, fin-keeled, scow-type racing machines, though fast, were admittedly freaks, with many bad qualities from the standpoints of seaworthiness, strength, and durability. After *Reliance*, yachtsmen agreed that a measurement rule was necessary that would help produce seaworthy

craft which would last, after their Cup days, as good, practical yachts for cruising and racing. By the time Lipton challenged again for a race, in 1914, such a rule, devised principally by Nat Herreshoff, was in force. Its success is attested by the fact that *Resolute* and *Vanitie*, built for Cup defense that year, remained in service under various owners until the late 1930s.

War broke out while *Shamrock IV* was crossing the Atlantic in 1914 and she and the American defenders were laid up until 1920, when the Herreshoff-built *Resolute* was selected over *Vanitie* in the trials. The 1920 race marked a transition in Cup his-

This drawing from *The Graphic* in 1901 gives an idea of the enormous spectator fleets that followed the closely matched *Columbia* and *Shamrock II* off Atlantic Highlands.

tory. It was the first race in which amateur skippers and afterguards commanded the rivals—Charles Francis Adams as skipper of *Resolute* and William (later Sir William) Burton of *Shamrock IV*. It was the last America's Cup series off New York. It was the first in which the boats were built to measure under the Universal Rating Rule, though, for the last time, the higher-rated yacht still conceded time allowance to the smaller. It was also the first time Sir Thomas Lipton saw one of his beloved *Shamrocks* win even one race for the Cup, for *Resolute's* rigging failed in the first race and she was beaten by *Shamrock IV* in the second, although thereafter she took three straight and the series. The 1920 race also saw the last of the traditional gaff rigs with their huge topsails. Their rigs were relatively taller and narrower, with shorter booms and bowsprits, than those of earlier days, but the modern jib-headed or "marconi" rig was just being tried out, cautiously, on a few small racing yachts in 1920.

The modern era in America's Cup races really started in 1930, when the venerable Sir Thomas made his fifth and last attempt to "lift the ould mug," as he was wont to call it. Gone now were the gaff mainsails, huge topsails, and overhanging booms and bowsprits. Their places were taken by the lofty, all-inboard jib-headed rigs (though the present overlapping genoa jib and double or parachute-type spinnaker were yet to be developed). Gone were time allowances. The boats were designed to an agreed rating—76 foot or "Class J" under the Universal Rule—and the uninitiated public no longer was baffled by the anomaly of a yacht finishing first yet being defeated on corrected time. Gone, too, was Nat Herreshoff from the active designing field, though his old yard still built the Cup defenders of 1930 and 1934. A new team took over the defense: Harold S. Vanderbilt as skipper and syndicate managing owner and W. Starling Burgess, son of Edward Burgess, of *Puritan*, *Mayflower*, and *Volunteer* fame, as designer.

Although the financial crash of October, 1929, occurred between the acceptance of Lipton's fifth challenge and the year of the race itself, its full effect hadn't been felt, and even the kind of financial brains that figure in this most expensive of yacht-racing activities still thought of it as a temporary setback. Which explains why four new

Class J sloops were built that winter, all for New York Yacht Club syndicates. They were *Weetamoe*, designed by Clinton H. Crane, *Enterprise*, by Burgess; *Yankee*, by Frank C. Paine of the same Paine family that had combined with the elder Burgess in defending the Cup in the 1880s, and *Whirlwind*, by L. Francis Herreshoff, son of Captain Nat, who was still alive but beyond his designing days. The two former were built at the Herreshoff shops, the two latter at Lawley's in Boston.

Trial races that season had some surprising results. *Weetamoe* was consistently the most promising boat until almost the final trial series. *Enterprise*, smallest of the four, seemed at first to be outclassed, but Vanderbilt and Burgess kept improving her until, in the final trials, they came out on top. *Yankee* was the fastest of all under her own conditions of strong winds and rough water, but was not as consistent in lighter going. *Whirlwind*, biggest of the quartet, was an also-ran all season, but many qualified observers felt she was a potentially fast hull that suffered from less skillful management and sailing, and perhaps from some rig defects.

Vanderbilt, with Burgess and his crack amateur afterguard and professional crew, fought *Enterprise* through a tough trial series to selection and—an easier job—to victory over *Shamrock V* in three straight but by no means one-sided races. The trials and Cup races were sailed for the first time off Newport, Rhode Island, in open water free from heavy commercial traffic, though it took a dozen Coast Guard vessels to keep the swarming spectator craft clear of the racers.

Sir Thomas went home, disappointed for the fifth time in his efforts to "lift the ould mug," and some months later he died. He had been *the* challenger for the America's Cup for so long that people wondered if there would ever be another race for it, now that he was gone.

Reliance, the Herreshoff sloop of 1903, was the biggest (143 feet 8 inches over all, 16,160 square feet of sail) of the so-called "fin-keel scow" type of racing sloop. She showed her stern to anything that came along under sail, as she is doing here to one of her rivals in the 1903 trial races.

Shamrock II and *Columbia* jockeying for position before the start of one of the 1901 races. *Columbia* was the only yacht ever to defend the America's Cup twice—in 1899 and again in 1901, when she bested the new boats built to defend against the second Lipton challenge.

Nathanael Greene Herreshoff, "the Wizard of Bristol," was a genius who dominated the racing yacht design and building scene for nearly forty years—from the early 1890s down to the 1920s.

The Herreshoff plant at Bristol, R.I., produced hundreds of outstanding sailing, steam, and power yachts. This photo was taken in the 1900s.

The little man with the big mustache. Captain Charles Barr was without doubt the most famous and successful of the professional racing skippers—and the last of them to command a Cup defender.

"Norwegian steam." Captain Barr's magnificently trained crew of Scandinavians hoists *Reliance's* huge mainsail.

No sailor himself, Sir Thomas Lipton watched his sloop race from the deck of his steam yacht *Erin,* as he is doing here. His personality, coupled with a flair for public relations and showmanship, made him the beau ideal of a yachtsman in the minds of the general public. Among non-yachtsmen, America's Cup events were still often called "the Lipton races" for many years after his death, which came soon after the 1930 races in which his *Shamrock V* was beaten by *Enterprise,* designed by Starling Burgess and sailed by Harold S. Vanderbilt.

Reliance shows the way to *Shamrock III* in a 1903 race start.

The closest thing to a winner Sir Thomas ever had was *Shamrock IV*, shown here in a commanding position on *Resolute's* weather bow. The yachts were built for a match in 1914, which was not held until 1920 due to the outbreak of World War I while *Shamrock* was sailing across the Atlantic. *Shamrock IV* won the first two races, but *Resolute* won the next three straight, and the match. This was the first America's Cup match in which the skippers were amateur yachtsmen; Charles Francis Adams sailed *Resolute* and Sir William Burton, *Shamrock IV*.

Hoisting the club topsail on *Shamrock III*. It required a couple of agile men aloft to handle these huge kites. The third *Shamrock*, in 1903, painted white with a green "boottop" along her waterline, was the only exception to Lipton's having his sloops' topsides painted a bright Irish green.

right:

One of the many Vanderbilt-Burgess innovations on *Enterprise* was the "Park Avenue" boom. The foot of the mainsail slid across the boom on tracks and slides. Its object was to give the foot of the sail a proper airfoil shape.

left:

Perhaps the ultimate development of the gaff-headed sloop rig, with its huge club topsail, was seen in *Resolute,* snapped here with everything drawing beautifully on a fairly close reach, and in her rivals of 1914 and 1920, *Vanitie* and *Shamrock IV.*

The interior of *Enterprise* looked like what it was—an ef-
ficiently equipped workshop. Some of these winches were
hand-me-downs from *Resolute, Vanitie,* and even from *Reliance* and her contemporaries. Later Class J boats were required to have crews' and owners' living quarters installed.

W. Starling Burgess, designer of two America's Cup defenders and co-designer of a third. He designed *Enterprise* in 1930 and *Rainbow* in 1934 for New York Yacht Club syndicates, and was co-designer with Olin Stephens of *Ranger* in 1937.

Enterprise in one of her early-season shakedown races in 1930. Out on her weather quarter are the old rivals of the 1914 and 1920 trials, *Vanitie* and *Resolute,* which were refitted as "trials horses" for the four new Class J America's Cup candidates of 1930. In a summer of hard, close racing *Enterprise* won an uphill campaign for the selection against *Weetamoe, Yankee* and *Whirlwind.*

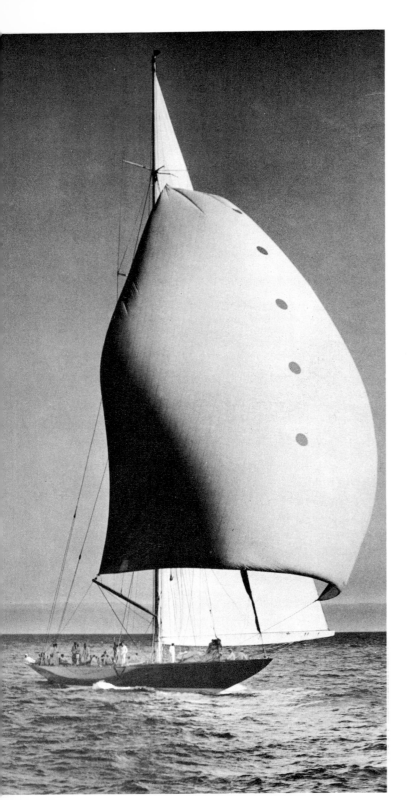

The

Great Days

of the

J - Boats

SIR Thomas Lipton's reign as undisputed thirty-year champion of Britain's efforts to regain the America's Cup was succeeded after his death much more quickly than expected, by another British yachtsman who had his eye on the trophy. Thomas O. M. Sopwith, unlike Lipton, was a racing yachtsman of considerable experience and, as one of England's leading aircraft manufacturers, he could well afford to go after the Cup. Wealth was no mean consideration. It cost a great deal to build a Class J sloop and cover her racing expenses for the season: sails and gear (much of it experimental), keep and wages of a crew of twenty-odd professionals, a power tender, a big diesel yacht to house the afterguard, and other incidentals. Such figures

After Sir Thomas Lipton's death following the 1930 series, a new America's Cup challenger appeared. British aircraft manufacturer T. O. M. Sopwith came over in 1934 and again in 1937 with two fine Class J sloops designed by Charles Nicholson, *Endeavour* and *Endeavour II*. The double-clewed or parachute-type spinnaker had come to stay, but the row of holes down the middle, shown here in *Endeavour's* spinnaker, which was supposed to give improved performance, proved a passing fad.

are rarely made public, even roughly, but one of the four syndicates of 1930 spent well over $900,000 by the time the selection trials—which their boat didn't win—were over.

The Sopwith challenge was duly accepted and Charles E. Nicholson, England's leading designer of large yachts, was commissioned to build the challenger. Nicholson had designed Sir Thomas Lipton's last two *Shamrocks* and was familiar with the kind of boats successful under the New York Yacht Club's Universal Measurement Rule. His choice as designer was no mistake. *Endeavour* was a beautiful thing, and unquestionably the fastest Class J sloop of her time.

With the country fighting its way out of a depression, there was only one new defense candidate in 1934. One boat was financed by a syndicate, again headed by Harold S. Vanderbilt. She was designed by Starling Burgess and built at the old Herreshoff plant at Bristol—no longer owned by the Herreshoffs now, but retaining much of the old management and skilled craftsmanship.

A couple of the older J-boats were still available as trial horses and possibly serious competitors. In fact *Yankee*, somewhat improved since 1930 and handled by the old master, Charles Francis Adams, came very close indeed to beating the new *Rainbow* in the final selection trials. Vanderbilt's able afterguard and professional crew and the Burgess skill at making *Rainbow* go faster, pulled her through.

It was the closest the New York Yacht Club has ever come to losing its cherished America's Cup. It was a four-out-of-seven series. *Endeavour* won the first race by two minutes, the second by 51 seconds, and left little doubt in anyone's mind—least of all in Vanderbilt's—that she was a faster boat than *Rainbow*. In the third race the British sloop was even farther ahead when, on the last leg, she ran into a "flat spot"—a local area where there was little or no wind. Sopwith made the tactical error of tacking to try to get out of it, and only got in worse. Vanderbilt held his course and ghosted through the flat. With Sherman Hoyt at the wheel, exerting his matchless genius as a helmsman, *Rainbow* picked up a little more breeze in the last few miles and won by over three minutes.

After that fatal error in judgment, *Endeavour* seemed to go to pieces. She was still the faster boat, but her people made tactical errors and were relatively slow in handling and trimming sails. Vanderbilt, a fine sailor and an even better organizer with a top-notch afterguard and a perfectly trained crew, made no mistakes, and he won the remaining three races.

It was a series that tried nerves and tempers. *Endeavour* finished one day with a red protest flag flying. Sopwith had luffed his boat to prevent *Rainbow* passing him to windward and claimed that Vanderbilt had failed to respond to the luff, as the rules required under the circumstances as Sopwith saw them. The committee declined to hear the protest, on a technicality—Sopwith had failed to display his protest flag immediately after the incident. The committee took a good deal of abuse for that, but it finally came out that they, from their bridge, had seen *Endeavour* clearly commit a foul on *Rainbow* in the tense maneuvering for position before the start. Had it come to a protest hearing, they would have had to rule the challenger out of the race before the later incident took place. They felt that of two evils—disqualifying Sopwith or taking the blame themselves for refusing to hear the protest—the latter would cause less hard feeling.

There were hard feelings aplenty as it was, but Sopwith was no Lord Dunraven. Three years later he was back with another Nicholson boat—in fact he brought both *Endeavours,* early in the season, and held his own "trial races" off Newport. *Endeav-*

our II was faster than her predecessor, but not fast enough.

That year Vanderbilt assumed the whole cost of building a boat. Burgess and a rising young naval architect, Olin J. Stephens, collaborated on a design. Four models were cut and tried, making use of newly developed model tank-testing techniques at Stevens Institute of Technology, which had been founded by, and named for, the Stevens family of *America* fame. The model that tested best became *Ranger,* the fastest of the Class J sloops.

She was built at the Bath (Maine) Iron Works—the first yacht built anywhere but at Bristol to defend the Cup since the 1880s. She started in hard luck, losing her 165-foot duralumin mast while under tow at sea on the night she left the builder's yard. But that was about her only bad luck—and bad enough considering the probable replacement cost. Once rerigged, she started showing her heels to the older J-boats in a manner that left no doubt as to who the defender would be.

Nor was there much doubt about who was going to win the America's Cup match itself after the first few miles of the first race between *Ranger* and *Endeavour II. Ranger* won that race by the sizable margin of 17 minutes, 5 seconds and took the match in four straight. The challenger managed to close the gap down to 3 minutes, 37 seconds in the last race. It was such a one-sided series that no dispute was possible. For *Ranger* turned out to be a boat without equal. From her first race she seemed the fastest, the most powerful, the most beautiful, and the most destined to win. As the racing season went on and it was shown that there was no competition for her, it seemed difficult to believe that a better J-boat could be built. We shall probably never know.

Rainbow crosses the bow of her trial horse, the old *Vanitie,* built in 1914.

right:

Rainbow, the 1934 defender, was considered by most keen observers of the series a slower boat than Sopwith's *Endeavour.* The latter won the first two races, but from then on the superior handling of Harold Vanderbilt and his afterguard and crew, plus a little bit of luck in the pinches, pulled *Rainbow* through to victory in the series.

left:

The masts of *Enterprise, Rainbow,* and *Ranger* were of duralumin. The standing rigging of the latter two were solid bars of the same material, light but enormously strong. Here a crew member adjusts the tension on a lower-shroud turnbuckle.

below:

Just before the battle. Jogging under easy sail in a light breeze, a few minutes before the start of one of the 1934 races, the skippers plan their strategy for being in position when the gun goes off. Here Tom Sopwith, at the helm of *Endeavour,* keeps an eagle eye on the maneuvering of *Rainbow,* while the British crew handles its sheets in relaxed pre-race fashion.

Page 154. Last and fastest of the Class J sloops was Harold Vanderbilt's *Ranger,* of 1937. On the wind in a breeze, these great sloops gave an unforgettable sense of surging power.

Page 155. From any angle *Endeavour* was one of the handsomest Class J sloops ever built.

The New York Yacht Club cruise which followed the Cup races of 1937 was the last great meeting of the Class J sloops. Nearest the camera is *Yankee,* unsuccessful 1930 and 1934 candidate but holder of the Cup boat record of 2 hours, 47 minutes, 59 seconds over a 30-mile triangular course. To windward of her are *Endeavour II, Ranger,* the first *Endeavour,* and *Rainbow.* The double-clewed jibs were characteristic of the Js that year.

The team that defended the America's Cup three times—Starling Burgess and Harold Vanderbilt.

Dousing the jib—old style and new. It took a lot of men out on the bowsprit to take in the jibtopsail of one of the big Cup defenders of half a century ago. The knockabout-rigged cup defenders of later years had all headsails inboard, like *Rainbow*. But there were other complications. Here a jib hank snapped itself over both of her double headstays and the sail wouldn't come down any farther until Rod Stephens shinned up there and unfouled it.

Postscript: The New Challenge

TWENTY years have elapsed since the 1937 races—the greatest length of time that the Cup has been unchallenged since the *America's* owners brought it home from Cowes. World War II broke out in 1939 and by the time it was over, racing yachts the size of Class J sloops were extinct. *Ranger* was 135 feet long on deck, with an 87 foot waterline, 21 foot beam, 15 foot draft, displacement of 166 tons, and carried 7,546 feet of sail. Income taxes consume the kind of incomes that used to support such yachts, while costs have skyrocketed to two and three times their former heights. All the American J Class sloops—even the matchless *Ranger*—were scrapped for their metal in wartime. The two *Endeavours* are reportedly still extant, bereft of their rigs and ballast keels, serving as houseboats.

Many propositions have been made since 1945 for reviving the America's Cup races. The ideas have ranged from an ocean race around Bermuda and back in cruising yachts to team races in 14-foot sailing dinghies. But the Deed of Gift, altered twice previously to allow for changing yachting customs, specified 65 feet waterline as the minimum size for yachts eligible for Cup matches. And responsible yachtsmen, here and abroad, felt that the tradition of competition for the Cup among the largest class of racing yachts active at the time of the races should be maintained.

In 1956, feelers were extended from England and a series of unofficial talks on the subject began. In order to expedite the return of Cup racing, the New York Yacht Club applied to the courts and the Deed of Gift was legally altered in two respects. The minimum waterline limit was lowered to 44 feet. And the requirement that a challenger must sail from her home port to the scene of the races on her own bottom was deleted. This had been a serious handicap to the challengers in time and expense more profitably spent in tuning up and trial races.

In May, 1957, a challenge for the America's Cup was received and accepted by the New York Yacht Club. The challenge came from the Royal Yacht Squadron, which originally sponsored the Hundred Guineas Cup—known as the America's Cup since 1851—and the race at which it was won. The challenge specified that the races be held between yachts of the 12-Meter Class, built under the International Rule of Measurement. A typical 12-Meter sloop's dimensions are 69 feet, 7 inches over all, 45 foot waterline, 12 foot beam, 8 foot, 11 inch draft and 1,916 square feet of sail. That's a far cry from the dimensions of a J-boat—but there are no J-boats any more.

There are 12-Meters racing in England and America today. Excepting a few slightly bigger ocean racing craft, they are the largest active racing yachts afloat. They are the contemporary heirs of the America's Cup tradition, which required the ultimate in design and performance of succeeding generations of yachting.

The *America's* owners presented the trophy to the care of the New York Yacht Club as a "perpetual challenge Cup for friendly competition between foreign countries." After twenty dormant years the America's Cup will soon be in circulation again, with racing off Newport, Rhode Island, between the biggest and best of today's British and American yachts.

The Class J sloops and other yachts of their size have passed into history. Soaring costs and high income taxes have killed them. After 21 years on the shelf, the America's Cup is being raced for again in 1958, but in smaller yachts—though still by the biggest active racing craft of their time. The 1958 races will be in 12-Meter Class sloops, not much more than half the over-all length of the Js. Typical of these yachts is *Vim*, which was built in 1939 for Harold S. Vanderbilt, who campaigned her successfully in England that year. Newest American Twelve until the building started for the 1958 races, *Vim* will doubtless take part in the 1958 trials, as *Resolute* and *Vanitie* did in 1930. Conceivably—though not likely—she might, like *Columbia* of 1899 and 1901, beat the new boats and be named as the defender.

4

4

OCEAN RACING
AND CRUISING

Across the Atlantic

THERE are many types of sailing yachtsmen, enjoying many varieties of yachting. Beyond the fact that they all like to sail boats on water, their aims are often very different. The man who races his one-design or restricted class sailboat around closed courses (on as many afternoons as he can get away from work during the season) enjoys the thrill of tense, constant, neck-and-neck competition. His sport is a brief contest of his boat's speed and his own skill against the speed and skill of his rivals.

The temperamental opposite of the afternoon racer is the leisurely, long-range cruiser. He cares nothing for competition but enjoys sailing, with or without congenial companions, for long days at sea; for a visit to a distant port; for a voyage around the world, perhaps. The ports are incidental, it's the sea in all its moods that this sailor loves. He is usually in no hurry and the sea-keeping ability of his boat, not her speed, is her most important feature to him.

The ocean racing man is another type of yachtsman, who combines these approaches to the sport. He likes the sea and long voyages on it. He and his boat can face weather as it comes—calm or gale, sunny skies or cold, penetrating rain and spray. But he is also a competitor at heart, whose enjoyment of his voyage is greatly enhanced by the prospect of arriving first at his destination. To do so he must keep his boat sailing at her best possible speed under varying conditions, day and night, for days or perhaps weeks on end. This takes stamina and unflagging determination, particularly when, as often happens, there are no rivals in sight to spur him on—though he knows there may be dozens just over the horizon.

THE GREAT OCEAN YACHT RACE.
BETWEEN THE HENRIETTA, FLEETWING & VESTA.
THE "GOOD BYE" TO THE YACHT CLUB STEAMER "RIVER QUEEN," 4 MILES EAST OF SANDY HOOK LIGHT SHIP DEC.R 11TH 1866.

The ocean racing yachtsman is, perhaps, the spiritual descendant of the old clipper captain. The clipper captain drove his ship with a relentless determination to break records and win commercially profitable voyages from his equally determined colleagues. He raced for the sport of it as well. He could win a silk hat from the skipper of some other ship that cleared at the same time from Melbourne, or the Golden Gate, or Calcutta as both headed for the same port with similar cargoes. Without the cares or the incentives of commercial enterprise to spur them on, however, ocean-going yachtsmen retain much of the romance of the clipper days.

Trans-Atlantic racing was started in 1866 when Pierre Lorillard, owner of the 105-foot centerboard schooner *Vesta*, and the

The first trans-Atlantic race. The schooners *Fleetwing*, *Vesta*, and *Henrietta* (left to right in this picture of them shortly after the start off New York), all about 106 feet long over all, started on December 11, 1866. Spinnakers were barred in deference to the anticipated December North Atlantic weather, but squaresails were carried. The stakes were $30,000 a side; officers and crews were all professionals; only one owner went along —James Gordon Bennett of *Henrietta*. George and Franklin Osgood, of *Fleetwing*, and Pierre Lorillard, of *Vesta*, sat it out in New York—and paid Bennett his $60,000 when *Henrietta* won.

brothers George and Franklin Osgood, owners of the keel schooner *Fleetwing*, started bragging one day and wound up betting $30,000 a side on whose boat could beat whose from Sandy Hook lightship to England. The fact that yachts were sailed by professionals in those days and owners seldom braved the hardships of a deepwater passage probably encouraged them to agree to start on December 11th, when the Western Ocean is not likely to be at its pleasantest. James Gordon Bennett, who owned the schooner *Henrietta*, declared himself in on the bet and actually made the passage himself.

Much of the way across the three schooners "had it rugged," as a sailor would say. Eight days out, scudding off at night before a southwesterly gale, *Fleetwing* was boarded by a big sea that swept eight men overboard. Two got back aboard. After trying for hours to locate the other six, *Fleetwing* went on for England.

Vesta was the first of the trio to make a landfall, sighting the lights of the Scilly Isles at 6:55 Christmas Eve. *Henrietta* saw them just 50 minutes later. But, through bad pilotage on the remaining 200 miles to Cowes, *Vesta* sagged off to leeward, and *Henrietta* swept past her to win, completing the passage in 13 days, 21 hours, 45 minutes. *Fleetwing*, hard driven again after the search for her lost men, came into Cowes at midnight of Christmas Day, eight and a quarter hours behind the winner and forty minutes ahead of *Vesta*, whose local pilot had cost her the race. Captain "Bully" Samuels, famous for his fast passages in sailing packet ships between New York and the British Isles, had commanded *Henrietta*.

There were few major ocean matches in the years following the first deepwater race. The 124-foot schooner *Dauntless* lost two, one to the America's Cup challenger *Cambria* in 1870, from Daunt Head, Ireland, to Sandy Hook, and another to the schooner *Coronet*, Sandy Hook to Cork, Ireland, in 1887.

The next big race was in 1905. In that year the German emperor, an enthusiastic yachtsman, sponsored a most impressive "solid gold" cup for a race from New York

A two-time loser. Built at Mystic, Conn., in 1866, the 124-ft. over all *Dauntless* twice raced across the Atlantic. In 1870 she was beaten by just one hour, 17 minutes, from Gaunt Head, Ireland, to Sandy Hook by the America's Cup challenger *Cambria*. In 1887, getting old and leaky, she was beaten by the new and larger schooner *Coronet* from Sandy Hook to Cork, Ireland, by some 30 hours. The famous old packet-ship master, Captain "Bully" Samuels, commanded *Dauntless* in both these races. Her owner in 1870 was James Gordon Bennett, in 1887, Caldwell Colt.

to The Lizard lighthouse, on the south coast of England. In 1916, when the Kaiser became our Enemy Number One, this cup was melted down as a contribution to our war funds, and proved to be a few dollars' worth of cheap metal, well-gilded. But in its day, the cup was a prized trophy. Eleven yachts sailed the race, ranging in size and rig from the 108-foot schooner *Fleur de Lys* to the huge, three-masted, full-rigged ship *Valhalla*, 245 feet long. This race started in May, and all but one of the owners went along. Owners and guests were just passengers, however, as the yachts were still commanded and manned by professionals. The winner was the 185-foot three-masted schooner *Atlantic*, owned by Wilson Marshall and commanded by the redoubtable Captain Charles Barr, of America's Cup fame.

It was another windy passage, and Captain Barr drove *Atlantic* to her limit all the way. Legend has it that he drove her so hard in a gale one night that owner and passengers were on their knees below deck, praying.

Atlantic's passage in that race, 12 days, 4 hours, one minute, from Sandy Hook to The Lizard, is the fastest on record for any sailing vessel—yacht or clipper ship. Since there are few sailing vessels of her size, and

Endymion, owned by George Lander, one of *Atlantic's* rivals in the 1905 race, had previously made a passage of 13 days, 8 hours, Sandy Hook to The Needles, which was a record until *Atlantic* bettered it.

none of her speed, left in the world today, this record will probably stand for all time.

Atlantic, designed by William Gardner, made other, nonracing, Atlantic passages and was a much-admired yacht for another forty years, ending her active sailing career as a training ship for U. S. Coast Guard midshipmen during World War II. She deserved a nobler fate, but wound up as a tea and gift shoppe, grounded in the shallow waters of a New Jersey coast summer resort.

Between 1905 and 1928, when the next trans-Atlantic race was sailed, ocean racing changed considerably. Big schooners, professionally sailed, were on their way out as smaller yachts, commanded, navigated, and mostly manned by amateurs, became prevalent. Owners and crews had cut their deepwater teeth on Bermuda and other ocean races, and some were ready for a longer and more difficult test.

In 1928, therefore, when the King of Spain put up a cup for a race from New York to Santander, Spain, for yachts of unlimited size, the Queen of Spain sponsored one for yachts from 35 to 55 foot waterline length. This small class started a week before the

big boats, and the two class winners arrived in Santander on the same day, July 25th.

William B. Bell's 135-foot Herreshoff schooner *Elena,* commanded by John Barr (nephew of the famous Charles) won in the big class. The *Atlantic,* carrying considerably less sail than in her earlier, record-making days, was second, and three others straggled in over a period of several days.

In the smaller class, the new Burgess-designed *Niña,* sailed by Paul Hammond and his able crew of amateurs, scored a close victory over two semi-fisherman type schooners, *Pinta* and *Mohawk.* A fourth

Eleven yachts of widely assorted rigs and sizes started the race for the Kaiser's Cup from Sandy Hook in 1905.

The left picture, in which you see the smoke from the starting gun, was made at the moment of the start; the right a few minutes later. Note how in the interim *Atlantic* (the black three-master), a white schooner, and the yawl *Ailsa,* respectively third, fifth and sixth from the left when the gun was fired, have everything set and drawing and have moved out and left the others. The white square-rigged ship, the Earl of Crawford's *Valhalla,* largest vessel in the race, is still trying to shake out her squaresails. She finished two days behind the 60-foot-shorter *Atlantic.*

starter, *Rofa,* carried an untried freak rig and sank while under tow of a steamer after she had been dismasted off the Grand Banks and her crew brought to safety.

It was the last trans-Atlantic race for big yachts manned by professionals and the first of many for yachts commanded and sailed by amateur yachtsmen.

After the race to Spain, trans-Atlantic racing enjoyed a booming new popularity. In 1931, ten yachts, 45 to 74 feet on deck, raced from Newport, Rhode Island, to Plymouth, England. Eight of them were American, two were British, and they represented a wide variety of rigs and types. This race marked the beginning of a new era in deepwater yachting, for the winner was *Dorade,* a new yawl designed by Olin J. Stephens. *Dorade* was the forerunner of a new general type of ocean racer, destined gradually to supplant the predominant semi-fisherman schooner type of yacht.

With her twenty-three-year-old designer-owner, his younger brother, Roderick, Jr., their father and a rugged young crew driving her, the 52-foot *Dorade* risked the short, but cold and often stormy Great Circle course across the Grand Banks. She found more strong, fair breezes there than her rivals did in the lower latitudes, and she made Plymouth in a bit over 17 days—nearly two days ahead of the second and third boats, the much larger *Landfall* and *Highland Light.* She won by over three days corrected time from the cutter *Skäl,* which had also crossed in the high latitudes.

In 1935, six yachts started from Newport for Bergen, Norway, and five arrived there. Tragedy struck the sixth, *Hamrah,* when her owner, Robert R. Ames, was washed overboard off the Grand Banks. His two sons, Richard and Harry, were drowned

The great schooner *Atlantic,* winner of the Kaiser's Cup in the 1905 trans-Atlantic race and still holder of the sailing record from Sandy Hook to the Lizard light, of 12 days, 4 hours, 1 minute, 19 seconds.

trying to save him. The winner this time was the yawl *Stormy Weather*, which Stephens had designed as an improvement on *Dorade*. She was huskier, more powerful, and faster than his early craft. Under 54 feet long, *Stormy Weather* finished only five hours behind the scratch boat, the 72-foot ketch *Vamarie*, and won by nearly two days corrected time.

Vamarie's captain, Alexander Troonin, went overboard one black, windy night in mid-ocean, but quick thinking and action by the helmsman, Sherman Hoyt, and the crew brought him back aboard safely.

There have been a number of races from Bermuda to England or Germany, and two from Havana, Cuba, to Spain since 1935. But the next race from a United States port to Europe was that from Newport, Rhode Island, to Marstrand, Sweden, in 1955. Of seven starters, four hailed from West German ports, two from the United States, and one from Norway. The winner was the 53-foot yawl *Carina*, designed by Philip L. Rhodes and owned and commanded by Richard S. Nye, of Greenwich, Connecticut.

Veteran seagoing yachtsmen shook their heads when *Carina* started, for she was an untried boat, just out of the builder's yard. Some of her sails had not even been hoisted before the race. But she fooled them—the only mishap reported by Dick Nye was the failure of her pump toilet—sailed the 3,450 miles in 20 days, 9 hours, 17 minutes and won by a good margin on corrected time, with the German yawl *Kormoran* second. *Carina* is a fine example of the combination keel-centerboard yawl which has been increasingly popular and successful in the ocean racing fleets since World War II. It combines wide beam, great sail-carrying power, and ample living accommodations with speeds equal to or better than those of the narrower and deeper models dominating the winning lists since the early 1930s.

Carina and Dick Nye did it again in 1957,

in a race from Newport to Santander, Spain, the finish point of the 1928 race. This race saw a Cuban, a German, a Swedish and four American yachts start. Dr. Luis H. Vidana's 66-foot yawl *Criollo*, from Cuba, scratch boat of the fleet, sailed the course in 19 days, 5 hours, 14 minutes, which compared to the 1928 race was about four days, 16 ½ hours faster than *Niña's* time over the 100-mile-longer course from New York and only two days, 9½ hours slower than that of the 135-foot over all *Elena*. But only eight hours after *Criollo*, in came *Carina*, with a time allowance which brought her corrected time down almost a day shorter than *Criollo's*.

Carina had beaten two higher-rating boats, the German *Hamburg VI* and the Swedish *Kay*, boat for boat, and as time allowances ran out on the three smaller American yachts, *Figaro*, W. T. Snaith, *White Mist*, G. W. Blunt White, and *Alphard*, Curtis Bok, *Carina* settled back on her anchor in Santander harbor to enjoy the distinction of being the first yacht to have won two trans-Atlantic races.

The North Atlantic has been the race-course for seagoing yachts and yachtsmen for more than ninety years. But these races have been few and far between, for it is a rare yachtsman with the right combination of inclination, time, money, and the requisite seamanship for such a race. Thus a trans-Atlantic race is an experience that sets a yachtsman, or a yacht, among the elite of the sport. Many more sailors might like to race across oceans but, for one reason or another, settle for shorter ocean races. The chief shorter races are those to Bermuda, Fastnet Rock, Rio de Janiero, and the 2,000-mile California-Hawaii race, which approaches the trans-Atlantic course in distance but is generally sailed under easier and more pleasant weather conditions than those which usually beset the "Western Ocean."

Dorade, something brand-new in ocean racers in those days, scored an outstanding victory in the 1931 race to England. Compared with the typical ocean racers of her day, she was deep and narrow of hull, showing the influence of the International Rule racing type, and her all-inboard yawl rig contrasted with the then popular schooners. Designed, owned, and in this race commanded by Olin J. Stephens, *Dorade* is generally regarded as the forerunner of the ocean-racing type of yacht that supplanted the semi-fisherman schooner type.

The rig that failed. William F. Roos's *Rofa* started the 1928 race to Spain under this novel and completely untried rig. Three booms, pivoting on wire stays that came down from the heads of her light, raking masts, each carried two tall, narrow sails, as the picture shows. It was aerodynamically ingenious but engineeringly unsound. She was dismasted off the Grand Banks and later sank while in tow of a steamer which took off her crew.

Niña, 59-foot over all, was designed by Starling Burgess for owner Paul Hammond for the 1928 Queen of Spain's Cup race, which she won handily. She had one of the first outstandingly successful staysail schooner rigs. Twenty-eight years later, *Niña* won the Class A trophy in the 1956 Bermuda Race. She is one of very few schooners still competing successfully in big-time ocean racing, with some minor modernization by her present owner, DeCoursey Fales, on the basic rig of 1928, shown here.

Stormy Weather, winner of the race from Newport, R. I., to Norway in 1935, was an improvement on *Dorade*, and her 1935 ocean crew was headed by Rod Stephens, Jr. Both these yawls are still winning prizes now and then, *Dorade* having done well in trans-Pacific races to Hawaii.

Start of the race to Norway in 1935. The boats nearest the camera are the 72-foot staysail ketch *Vamarie*, scratch boat and first to finish, and *Stormy Weather*, corrected time winner. The old three-master at the right (not in this race) is the *Azara*, last to finish (27 days) in the 1928 race to Spain.

One of the few tragedies of ocean racing history.
In the Newport-to-Norway race of 1935 Robert
E. Ames (left) was swept overboard from his ketch
Hamrah by a huge wave south of the Grand Banks.
In trying to rescue him, by swimming and with a
small dinghy, his two sons, Richard and Harry
(second and third from left) were drowned with
him before the ketch, crippled by the breaking
of her main boom as she jibed around, could ma-
neuver to pick them up. The other three boys of
the crew, Charles Tillinghast, Jr., Roger Weed
and Sheldon Ware, finally worked the ketch back
to port.

Typical of today's popular beamy, moderate-draft combination keel-centerboard ocean racers is Richard S. Nye's Phillip
Rhodes-designed *Carina*, winner of the 1955 race to Sweden
and the 1957 race to Spain. These yawls are a distinct departure from the fashion of narrow keel ocean racers set by
Dorade and *Stormy*, being stiffer in strong winds and much
roomier below decks.

Racing to Bermuda

FEW yachtsmen have the time, or can afford the expense, to take part in trans-Altantic races, but many thousands gratify their love for seagoing competition in deep-water races of shorter duration. The most famous of such races are those held, off and on for the past fifty years, from northern Atlantic Coast ports to Bermuda—true open ocean courses of from 628 to 675 miles, depending on the starting point.

Beginning with only three boats in 1906, this race has built up in popularity until the record fleet of 1956 numbered eighty-nine entrants. Allowing an average of about seven men per boat, more than six hundred yachtsmen (and a few yachtswomen) would take part in such a race—at least 90 per cent of them amateurs.

The race has been the inspiration and more or less the model for many others. In this country we have the 2,000-mile trans-Pacific race from southern California to Hawaii (which started in the same year as the Bermuda race and drew fifty-three boats in 1955); the Mackinac races of the Great Lakes; the Southern Circuit races from Florida ports to Nassau and Havana; the East Coast's Manchester, Massachusetts, to Halifax, Nova Scotia, and Annapolis, Maryland, to Newport, Rhode

Island, events; the West Coast race to Acapulco, Mexico, and a host of others. England has its notoriously tough-weather Fastnet Rock race and a number of races across the English Channel to continental ports; the Baltic has its "Around Gotland Island" race. The "Blue Ribbon of the South Atlantic" is sailed for every third year from Buenos Aires, Argentina, to Rio de Janiero, Brazil. "Down under," the hard-bitten sailors of Australia and New Zealand race across some of the stormiest stretches of ocean that any yachtsmen could face. Perhaps the best known of all these, however, are the Bermuda races.

In the early years of the century Thomas Fleming Day, a hard-bitten deepwater sailor who edited the magazine *The Rudder*, did a good deal of needling of his readers and fellow yachtsmen on the theme that, while they made a lot of salty talk about the seagoing qualities of their boats and themselves, they rarely made voyages more daring than a few days' runs within sight of land.

The upshot was that in 1906 three small yachts raced from Gravesend Bay, New York, to Bermuda, the winner was the 38-foot over-all yawl *Tamerlane*, owned and commanded by Frank Maier. It took her about five and a half days—not bad time for a boat of under 40 feet. And it is interesting to note that *Tamerlane,* designed and built by Larry Huntington, is still actively cruising on Long Island Sound, and looks surprisingly youthful.

That started it. Next year twelve yachts raced, with H. A. Morss's 85-foot schooner *Dervish* winning in the large class and Richard D. Floyd's 40-foot yawl *Lila* in the small. Only five yachts started from Marblehead in 1908. The prizes went to *Dervish* and E. J. Bliss's 65-foot schooner *Venona.* Five raced again from New York in 1909, George S. Runk's 93-foot schooner *Margaret* winning; but in 1910 there were only two entrants, with Harold S. Vanderbilt successful in the 76-foot schooner *Vagrant.* Thereafter the sport lapsed until 1923.

Again it was a magazine-editing sailor, Herbert L. Stone of *Yachting,* who was the sparkplug, pointing out in print that the semi-fisherman type yachts that had become popular since the end of World War I were ideally suited for deepwater passages and it was time some of them tried the Bermuda course. Mr. Stone and a group of friends, independent of any American club but with the blessing of the Royal Bermuda Yacht Club, organized and started a race. Twenty-two yachts, ranging from fisherman schooners to conventional racing craft, started from New London, Connecticut, and in spite of the very heavy weather, there were no mishaps. Owner-designer John G. Alden in his schooner *Malabar IV* took the trophy.

Though the rules and conditions have been highly developed since, that race set the general pattern in force today. Only yachts from about 35 to 72 feet long are eligible, and the master and navigator must be amateurs, although there are generally a few paid hands on the larger boats. The simple time-for-length handicap of 1923 has developed into a scientific and successful speed-formula rating rule, now used by many clubs for many races. The committees require certain standards of seaworthiness of yacht and gear, designed to prevent accidents, and in the history of the races only two boats have been lost—one by fire and one by stranding—and only one life lost.

The fleet shrank to fourteen in 1924, when Robert N. Bavier won in his yawl-rigged, 40-foot-waterline *Memory.* It appeared that every year was too often to hold a race of this kind, and since then they have been held biennially, except during the war years.

The Cruising Club of America, founded in 1922, took over the management of the Bermuda races in 1926, when there were sixteen starters, and John Alden showed them the way again in his new *Malabar VII.* In 1928, with twenty-five starting, the victor was another yawl-rigged Forty, Russell Grinnell's *Rugosa II.* The 1930 race had forty-two starters and a winner from the semi-fisherman type schooner ranks, Dr. R. W. Ferris's *Malay,* a Class B boat of 45 feet.

The 1932 race was notable in several respects. The financial crisis cut the fleet to 27 sail, while the weather conditions—strong reaching breezes all the way—made for fast passages. The 62-foot sloop *Highland Light,* sailed by her designer, Frank C. Paine, went from the Montauk Point starting buoy to the finish line off St. David's Light, Bermuda, a distance of 628 miles, in 71 hours, 35 minutes, 43 seconds. This record time was unbeaten for twenty-four years. Although potentially faster boats

The fisherman-type schooners, gaff-rigged and some "baldheaded" (i.e., without topsails, like *Black Hawk* at the right), made up the bulk of the 1923 Bermuda Race fleet, a part of which is shown here starting off New London. Others were conventional yacht types like Bob Bavier's *Memory,* the white yawl here, which was first to finish but lost out that year on corrected time. (She won the next year's race, however.) *Memory* was a rerigged New York Forty.

Racing fisherman. The Gloucester fishing schooners, in the days before diesel engines replaced sails on the fishing banks, were a magnificent type of fast, able sailing craft, built to make fast trips to and from market and take any weather that came, summer or winter. It was these vessels that inspired the so-called fisherman or semi-fisherman type of yacht developed by John G. Alden, William H. Hand, Charles D. Mower, William Roué, and other designers; a type that dominated ocean racing for the first decade after the revival of the Bermuda races in 1923. In this picture the *Elizabeth Ann Howard*, Captain Ben Pine, is seen from the deck of the *Henry Ford*, Captain Clayton Morrissey. The *Ford* beat the *Howard* in these trial races but lost to the *Bluenose*, Captain Angus Walters, of Lunenburg, Nova Scotia, in the International Fishermen's Races of 1922.

sailed during those years, the conditions were never again as good. John Alden won on corrected time with *Malabar X*, making him the only owner-skipper in the fifty-year history of the race to earn the Bermuda Trophy three times. It was in this race that the first yacht to be lost, the schooner *Adriana*, burned on her first night out, but all but one of her crew were rescued by the British cutter *Jolie Brise*. Spontaneous combustion in an oilskin locker behind a hot cabin stove caused the fire. Clarence Kozlay, helmsman at the time, stuck to his post, holding the burning ship on course until all his shipmates had leaped to safety aboard *Jolie Brise*, which by then had drifted so far away that Kozlay's own jump fell short and he was drowned.

A change in the character of the fleet also began to manifest itself in 1932. The semi-fisherman schooner was still the typical entry but newer boats, with slightly faster hulls and taller, jib-headed yawl and sloop rigs, such as *Highland Light* and *Dorade* (which won Class B that year), had begun to take over. One of these, Rudolph J. Schaefer's Sparkman-and-Stephens-designed *Edlu*, won in 1934, when the fleet began to grow again, with twenty-nine starters. Forty-four started the next year but ten of them gave up and returned to port when they met the hardest easterly gale the Bermuda Race has ever had to contend with. Surprisingly, the winner in that storm-swept contest was one of the smaller boats, Robert P. Baruch's Rhodes-designed sloop *Kirawan*.

A new champion began her reign in 1938. The 72-foot yawl *Baruna*, owned by Henry C. Taylor and designed by Sparkman and Stephens, was first to finish and winner in the fleet on corrected time, a triumph she was to repeat in 1948. In 1946 (the only intervening race because of World War II) *Baruna* finished first but lost the Bermuda Trophy to A. Howard Fuller's sloop *Gesture* on corrected time.

By 1950 the fleet had recovered from wartime setbacks and swelled to fifty-four starters, divided for the first time into three classes instead of into the former two, according to size. William T. Moore's yawl *Argyll* captured the Bermuda Trophy.

In 1952 began a series of victories by the smaller yachts, in the fleet corrected-time competition for the Bermuda Trophy. The winner was Richard S. Nye's yawl *Carina*, 46 feet long but in Class C, the small-boat third of the fleet. Two years later, with the 76-boat fleet divided into four classes, one of the smallest of the Class D boats, Daniel D. Strohmeier's 40-foot yawl *Malay*, beat all the other entrants on corrected time.

Carleton Mitchell's *Finisterre*, the 1956 Bermuda Trophy winner, was an even lower-rating craft, a 39-foot yawl of the beamy, moderate draft, combination keel-centerboard type. Yawls of this type are not only inherently fast but until now have enjoyed a slight advantage in rating which had been put into the rule back when the typical "fat" centerboarder was on the slow side. Yawls of similar type, Dick Nye's new and larger *Carina* and William T. Snaith's *Figaro*, likewise won in Classes B and C respectively in 1956, but by way of healthy contrast the Class A winner on corrected time was one of the few schooners left in serious ocean racing, DeCoursey Fales's *Niña*, which had won the race to Spain in her maiden year of 1928.

Highland Light's old Bermuda course record finally went by the board in 1956 when the 72-foot yawl *Bolero*, under the Swedish flag and command of her new owner, Sven Salen, made a passage of 70 hours, 11 minutes, 37 seconds over the

John G. Alden, master yacht designer and sailor, won his third Bermuda race with the schooner *Malabar X* in 1932. Of Alden's long succession of *Malabars*, the "Ten" represents perhaps the ultimate development of the semi-fisherman type.

635-mile course from Newport, Rhode Island, where the Bermuda races have been started since 1936. *Bolero* had been designed for John Nicholas Brown in 1949 by Sparkman and Stephens, as an improvement on *Baruna,* which is now owned on the West Coast. For the first time since 1932, prevailing strong fair winds had al-

lowed the big Class A yachts to make their best speeds for most of the course. The second boat to finish, H. G. Haskell, Jr.'s *Venturer,* also beat *Highland Light's* record by a few minutes.

One more record was set in 1956—the fleet numbered eighty-nine starters.

The old and the new in 1932. The yawl *Dorade* (right), forerunner of the modern ocean-racing type, plows through the lee of a typical gaff-headed fisherman-type schooner off Montauk Point at the start of the 1932 Bermuda Race.

It can get wet, between Newport and Bermuda. No longer do sailors—amateur or professional—have to swarm out on those long bowsprits the Gloucestermen used to call "widow-makers." But they can still get wet changing headsails. What goes up over the top of one sea is likely to come down smack-o into the middle of the next one, and the foredeck gang may get just a shade damp.

Highland Light, 62-foot cutter designed and at this time
sailed by Frank C. Paine, set a Bermuda Race record (71 hr.,
35 min., 43 sec.) in 1932 that stood for 24 years. She is now
sailed by U. S. Naval Academy midshipmen.

Queen of the Bermuda Race for a decade, Henry C. Taylor's
72-ft. yawl *Baruna*. She led the fleet across the finish line in
the 1938, 1946, and 1948 races; won the Bermuda Trophy
twice and was third on corrected time in 1946.

Off to Bermuda in a breeze of wind—the Class A start in 1946. Howard Fuller's *Gesture,* the dark sloop to windward (*foreground*), won the Bermuda Trophy that year.

It "breezed on" an hour or so after the start of the 1954 Bermuda Race from Newport, R.I., and Rod Stephen's crew in *Mustang* are shortening sail. "Rod's" crews are famous for how very few minutes it takes them to turn in a reef, when the wind pipes up enough so she'd go faster with less sail showing.

The fastest of them all. *Bolero* set the new course record to Bermuda, 70 hr., 11 min., 37 sec., in the 1956 race. Designed by Sparkman and Stephens and originally owned by John Nicholas Brown, she was owned and commanded by Sven Salen of Sweden in this race.

This shot of the Class B start in the 1948 Bermuda Race shows why old sailors complain that "all these modern ocean racers look alike."

Winning the 1956 Bermuda Race was a high point in the racing career of Carleton Mitchell's yawl *Finisterre*, which won 25 of the first 40 races she started in her first two years. Of Sparkman and Stephens design, she is of the highly successful centerboard type developed since World War II, which combines moderate draft and wide beam with a lead keel through which her centerboard works.

Life Under Sail

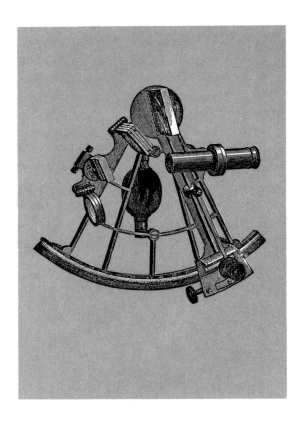

OCEAN racing is different from any other kind of sailing. The excitement of racing is sharpened by the open sea. When you're cruising—even cruising across an ocean—you can relax and enjoy life most of the time. You want to keep the ship going well, of course, but a few minutes here and there don't matter. If it looks like dirty weather coming up, you shorten sail well ahead of time, perhaps put the storm trysail on her before dark if indications point to a lot of wind coming before dawn. If it gets really rugged, you heave the ship to under riding sails, make sure she's riding easily and the gear is all in good shape, then go below and relax in your bunk, taking an occasional peek out the hatch to be sure things aren't going wrong on deck.

When the wind begins to ease, you jog along under easy sail for a while, just to be

sure it really means to stay fine; perhaps put off making full sail again until all hands have had a meal, or until the change of the watch when many hands will make light work of it.

Not so the ocean racer. He has a date somewhere over the horizon—a date he's always late for and rushing to make. And all around him—whether he can see them or not—are other boats and crews trying to make that same date ahead of him. He can't let up for a minute. The ship must be carrying all the sail she can use, and exactly the right sails, at all times. And the sails must be trimmed at exactly the right angle for the wind and the course, and frequently trimmed a bit harder, or eased, for every little shift and flaw in the wind, of which there are many times more, even in what passes for a steady breeze, than the landsman has any idea of.

If one of those dirty-looking Gulf Stream squalls comes looming up over the horizon, you don't shorten sail on the chance it might hit you—you lug your kites right up to the moment it strikes, with a man holding a turn on each halyard, ready to let go if he has to, or hang on if you think you can lug the sail through it. And the moment the wind eases, up go the big sails again, even if it looks as though another squall will hit you before the hour is out.

The keen ocean racer is on his toes all the time—his toes and his nerves. There is no lashing the helm and letting the ship sail herself in steady breezes—the helmsman must keep his eye shifting from sails to compass and back, getting the most out of the ship every minute. At least once an hour, in most ocean racers, a new helmsman, keen and keyed up, replaces the man who has been at the wheel, perhaps, long

As the rising sun silhouettes sails on the eastern horizon, the guessing starts. Who are those two? They weren't in sight last night. Have we over-hauled and weathered them during the night? Or did we dope off, and let them come up on us from astern?

Taking a little nap forward? Not a bit! He's "sight-ing" the luff of the big jib and calling back at intervals to the helmsman: "You're a little light!" —"Hard full!"—"Try her up a bit!" Constant, criti-cal sail-watching is vital if you want to win.

Breezing on. The crew takes the mizzen off the yawl to ease her a bit.

enough to get tired, careless, or slow in his reactions.

So far, there is little here that isn't equally true of the afternoon racing man. But while he keeps himself going at top competitive pitch for a few hours, after the finish he makes port to relax over a drink and dinner. The ocean racer, when his watch on deck is over, goes below to grab a bite, if it's mealtime, and then tries to sleep. To sleep in a narrow bunk that may be pitching and rolling like mad, if the sea is rough; that is pretty sure to be heeled over at an angle, and that may be soaking wet, in bad weather, from his own wet clothes or from those of some shipmate who slept there last watch.

He may get almost four hours' rest before someone shakes him and says, "On deck—eight bells coming up." Or he may be awakened at any moment by a yell for "All hands," if the weather turns bad, or something goes wrong on deck that the watch can't handle without help. So it goes on: four hours on watch—four hours below—four on—four off—for a couple of days, or a week, or maybe three or four weeks if you happen to be racing across an ocean.

The afternoon racer, too, has his competition always close by. He can gauge his own boat's performance by the way she is gaining or losing on other boats around him; he can see at once the effect of a slight change in trim; he may get into a fair slant

of wind, or avoid a bad one, by watching other boats nearby. The ocean racer may see no one for days on end. It's amazing how fifty yachts, bound from the same starting line to the same finish across a few hundred miles of ocean, can disappear from each other's view within a few hours of the start, and yet converge so closely at the end. It takes a special kind of effort to keep yourself and your crew driving the boat at top speed, watch after watch, when there's no competitor nearby. Having another yacht in sight, to try to overhaul or run away from, helps a lot, and it often develops, when an ocean race is over, that the winner was a boat that had one or more rivals of about her own size and speed within sight most of the way.

Ocean races don't stop at night, and getting the best speed out of a boat when you can't even see your sails takes a special kind of seamanship with a big dash of instinct in it. Many races are won at night. Most experienced ocean racers have acquired this skill, but thirty years ago, when this branch of the sport was new to most yachtsmen, there were a few skippers and crews particularly noted for being able to work out ahead in the hours of darkness. John Alden, who won three Bermuda races, was such a skipper and usually had such a crew.

It sometimes happens that an ocean racer may day after day be overhauled and passed by a larger and faster boat, which at dusk is hull-down ahead. But each following morning the racer's crew will look back and see the larger craft's topsail notching the horizon astern. The 24-hour crew of the smaller boat may sacrifice sleep, but it is a deprivation which pays off in added speed.

Ploughing into a strong head wind, with the lee rail dragging through solid water and the suds from the lee bow wave sloshing up into the foot of the genoa jib. It's thrilling, but she'll go faster, skipper, if you take off a little sail and get that rail out of the water.

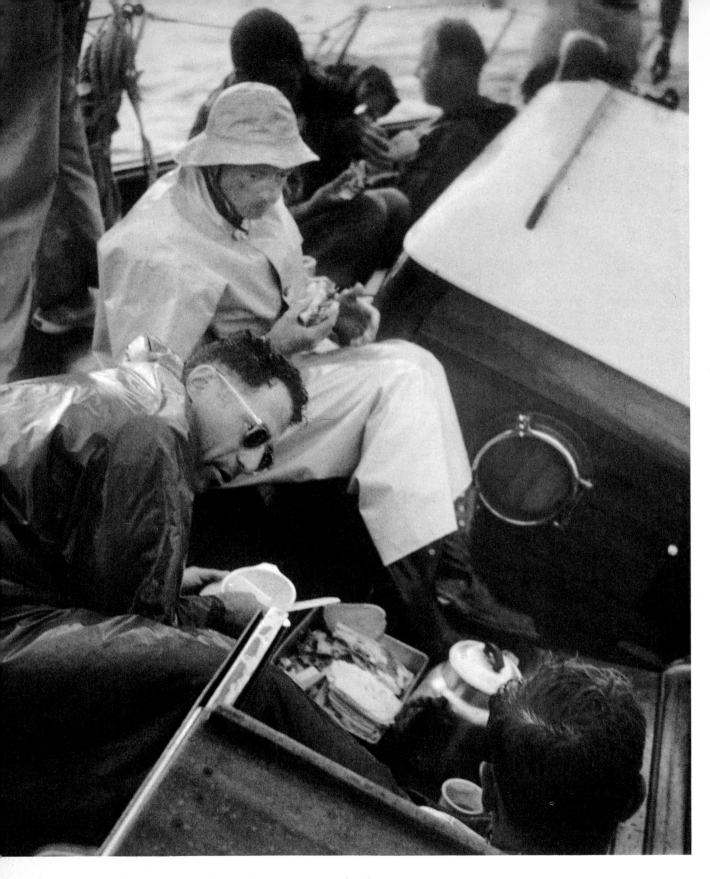

Chow on deck. The cook passes up sandwiches and coffee to the oilskinned watch on deck—and does it taste good!

Oilskins are a "must," for there's always some kind of a wet job to be done down in the lee scuppers.

The ocean racer has to be a handy man as well—at least a few on each boat do. If something serious goes wrong with your gear in an afternoon race, you get your boat to the shipyard and have the damage repaired next morning. If the same thing goes wrong at sea, you fix it yourself. Before you get where you're bound for, someone may have to shin aloft to fix an ailing stay or reeve a new halyard; you may have to sew up split and torn sails a dozen times; you may even have to rig a jury mast or rudder.

The afternoon racer can usually see his way from one buoy to the next, or at the most have to do a little simple piloting. The ocean racer depends on celestial navigation to get him to where he's going. The skipper and crew may do a perfect job of sailing the boat, but if the navigator doesn't get them to their goal by the shortest and fastest course it won't do them any good. The mathematical part of navigation is pretty simple today, with all the new books. Taking a sight from the bridge of a big ship is no great trick, either. But taking one from the deck of a small sailing yacht, pitching

Always a little job for the sailmaker. Light sails snag on things; seam stitching lets go; the man with the palm and needle cobbles it up before it has a chance to rip out seriously.

Even stainless-steel rigging stretches, and you have to set up a turn or two on the turnbuckle to keep the proper tension on shrouds and stays.

and rolling, dropping into the troughs of seas that tower over your head; throwing solid water all over you and your sextant—that's an art, especially when the sun is peeping out feebly at long intervals between wind-driven clouds, or the horizon under the stars at evening twilight is fuzzy with haze.

If the navigator raises your desired landfall right over the bow at the time he said you'd see it, he's quite the hero at the moment. But let him make one little slip, ever so unimportant, anywhere along the course, and he never hears the end of it. He's the man who lost the race; a handy scapegoat for the others to blame so they can forget all the things *they* should have done and didn't. And of course, navigators do make mistakes. More than one yacht has sailed right past low-lying Bermuda, just over the horizon, and on for a hundred miles before the error was discovered.

And last but not least, the cook. The man who, working in a cramped and overheated galley, half-smothered for lack of fresh air when the ship is battened down in wet going; tossed around like a pea in a rattle when the going is rough; pitched against a hot stove and dodging everything from scalding coffee to sliding cakes of ice when

"Slack an inch or two on that sheet, but don't let
it get away from you."

As soon as a spinnaker is doused, it has to be
stopped up again with "rotten twine" so it can be
hoisted and broken out the minute the wind fairs
again. A pleasanter job to do in this kind of weather
than on a black, windy night.

the motion is bad, hasn't much to do except turn out three or four square meals for a hungry crew, plus hot coffee and sandwiches for the change of the watch at midnight; keep the galley clean; and keep everybody's spirits up. Most of the best ocean racing cooks are amateurs—many pros wouldn't take the beating at any kind of wages.

Does all this make ocean racing sound grim? Well, it isn't. If you're one who loves ships and the sea, the fine days and nights, the congenial shipmates, and the thrill of competition outweigh any little discomforts, like solid water running down inside your oilskins while you battle to take in a flogging genoa jib in a screeching midnight squall. Either you like ocean racing or you don't. If you do, it's the greatest sport in the world.

The sun goes to bed in a low bank of cloud as another day at sea ends. It's calm now—just drifting along—but there may be wind in that sky and that yellow sun. Could be the call will come for "All hands on deck to shorten sail," along in the midwatch.

214

5

5

EVERYBODY

AFLOAT

Everybody Afloat

THE red, white and blue flag that flies gaily over the transom of water-borne craft all across the country is the American ensign, created by an act of Congress in 1848 as the distinguishing signal of an American yacht. The legislation authorized the Secretary of the Navy to design the flag, and the Secretary of the Treasury to license "Yachts used and employed exclusively as pleasure vessels, and designed as models of naval architecture." The august Senators and Congressmen of that year must have had some high hopes for the future of American yachting, and must also have believed that the Naval branch of the Government would have more interest in the sport than coming to the aid of yachtsmen in distress; for they were careful to include the clause, "Owners shall at all times permit the naval architects in the employ of the United States to examine and copy the models of said Yachts."

In 1870, the act was amended to grant Custom House privileges to "Yachts belonging to a regularly organized Yacht Club of any foreign nation which shall extend like privileges to the Yachts of the United States." For the identification of American Yachts and their owners who intended to sail in foreign countries, the amendment created "a commission to sail for pleasure in any designated Yacht belonging to any regularly organized and incorporated Yacht Club." By 1870, both the "Yacht" and the "Yacht Club" had received recognition in the statutes of the Federal Government. It would be interesting to know whether this was the first time the Federal Government recognized through statute, such specific means of organized pleasure.

To yacht club members, the club is the center about which the sport revolves. It may be a big, expensive, socially select organization, offering all sorts of club and community facilities, or a simple frame building on a dock where the boat owner can keep his gear and his dinghy, and meet a few pals. The larger ones may have all of the pleasures and problems peculiar to that way of club life, lavish entertainment, and social activities that have little connection with the sport of yachting. The smaller clubs may just provide the needed friendly and functional access and services necessary to the mooring of a boat—dock, water and parking facilities.

The yacht club has its characters too. There is the fellow who, as soon as he boards his twenty-foot sloop, treats his guests as though he was the captain of a

It takes a lot of skill (and usually a bit of luck) to get as good a start as No. 5003 has here, when 40 or more boats go over the line on a single gun. This is a Lightning Class start on Long Island Sound in very light air. The numerals and letters hoisted on the race committee boat signal the turning marks of the courses for the different classes.

clipper ship driving his crew to set a new speed record. There is the gadgeteer, who has the latest and finest of every kind of new device aboard, but treats them so carefully he never uses any of them; the fellow who seems to have so much fun fitting out that when he is ready to take his first sail it is just about time to haul out again. Then there are the ladies: the ones with such a keen knack for sailing, their husbands just go along for the ride; the girls who carry so much gear aboard the day is spent in stowing; and most of the feminine crew—bless them—who keep it a coeducational sport.

For the racing fraternity, the club provides the necessary organization, the regatta committee work that makes racing possible. As in all club activity the usual small group of dedicated people willing to do the staff work find plenty of it to do, and plenty of fellow members willing to let them do it all. The stars worn on the uniform of club officers mean toil and trouble as well as honor. One of the most rewarding sides of club life is the expanding development of junior sailing classes, with competent instruction and a racing program for the often surprisingly capable youngsters. Out of this pool of youthful talent emerges a good percentage of the winners of sectional and national competitions. There is a wide opportunity for annual competition in national or international championship racing in such classes as the Bantam, Beetle Cat, Comet, Lightning, Penguin, Moth, Sailing Dinghy, Raven, Snipe, Star, Thistle, 210, and others.

Racing craft constitute a small percentage of the number of yachts afloat, but a race is a dramatic spectacle which, once seen, is never forgotten. For years races have been the focus of attention for camera fan and artist, and the subject of most of the stories on yachting in the newspapers. As other aspects of boating become more popular, the emphasis on racing is changing, but its attractions as a competitive sport are very strong.

The racing man's preoccupation with sailing differs from the fellow who just sails for the fun of it, not so much in form as in intensity. It is not enough that his boat be in good condition—her hull, fittings and sails must be in top form. His crew must be not only good companions, but fast, skillful sail handlers and dependable helpers in every phase of the sailing game. On race day morning he has to motor down to the club, board his craft, bend the sails and move out to the starting area on time. The time spent sailing around before the preparatory gun is filled with friendly greetings to passing competitors, but he must also study the wind and weather, anticipate changes, evaluate tactics, and form judgments about the best starting position.

Each passing second takes on more meaning. What a few moments before looked like individual boats milling aimlessly about, arranges itself into a definite pattern. Speed and motion are judged in terms of the seconds before the gun, the starting line, and the position of the other starters. With the firing of the starting gun the race is on. A good skipper will already have anticipated that instant; will be free of interference from the other starters, and in the best position to cross the line on time, with full headway on and his wind clear.

If the start is to windward, the boats in more favorable positions may hold their courses; those less fortunate may come about to find a stronger or better slant of wind. The crisscross pattern of a fleet working to windward takes form, and as the sun shines on their wakes from high overhead it is like the flash of dueling swords. If the wind is strong, the crew hiking out on the weather rail is splashed with spray and knows the exhilaration of sailing on the sparkling wave, as well as the fight to win. If the breeze is light and variable, the smooth surface of the water marked with the soft ruffle of vagrant cat's-paws, the leading boats may know the maddening frustration of being becalmed in a flat spot while rivals they had left astern sail up alongside and the race starts over again.

The fellow out cruising can take the wind and wave as it comes. A lot of wind is a challenge, but in the absence of it, the engine will move him along. To him the pleasure is in going, and the variations in weather are spice to season the way. If he is so inclined his boat may have the best fittings, the newest gadgets, and a perfectly smooth coat of bottom paint, like a racing yacht, or she may have just the bare necessities to provide him with safety and the creature comforts. The boat provides comfort; the crew, companionship; the equipment, convenience and safety. That is how it should work out. But a boat is also a bundle of compromises. No boat is so designed that she can serve every purpose afloat equally well. A fast little day sailor can be a mighty uncomfortable cruising boat, and a big, beamy, comfortable river craft may be unmanageable at sea.

The experienced sailor finds his pleasure in a well-designed craft, used as it was intended to be. The elder J. Pierpont Morgan is reputed to have said, "If you have to ask what it costs to run a yacht, you can't afford one." Today it is possible for a budget-minded boatman to get afloat comfortably in a well-designed and well-built craft of any of the many types there are to choose from. Not very long ago, most yachts were custom-built. Modern methods of mass production, utilizing new materials and methods, make it practical to produce a large number of craft from a single design. Inboard-powered craft available as stock boats run from small utility runabouts through a whole gamut of cruiser types to those providing all-year-round living accommodation.

The old skills of shipbuilding are changing, too. The building of wooden yachts still requires special arts in carpentry and joinerwork, but the man behind the forming of thousands of small aluminum craft may be the operator of a large power press. In making molded plywood hulls one may lay sheets of veneer and glue over a mold, and in plastic hulls, layers of glass fabric and resin inside a form. In the 1890s, hollow masts were glued together with a mixture of quicklime and pot cheese. Milk products are still used to make binders, for many of the old things are still with us in a different form, but modern chemistry has produced,

in casein glues, a product far more adaptable and efficient in boatbuilding than pot cheese. The impact of the new synthetic materials has just begun to be felt in boatbuilding.

Mr. Morgan's reputed remark was in reference to a very large yacht, and there is nothing now to prevent a man from lavishing a fortune—if he has it—on a large yacht. There are other ways to the water, however, and in this do-it-yourself age most yachtsmen do much of the fitting out and maintenance work necessary on their boats, and find it fun.

In the early spring, for the more rugged yachtsmen, the flowering forsythia marks the beginning of the fitting out season. Less hardy souls wait for the leaves to appear. Then scraping, sanding, painting, and the general overhaul before launching begins in earnest. Some aspects of fitting out are almost as satisfying to the sailor as being afloat. To begin with, he is near the boat, and after a long winter its very presence is both a promise and a reward. The shipyard, if he is in one, has a restrained kind of expectancy, not quite like anything else. It is filled with other boats, and to a yachtsman every boat has a message and appeal of her own. The sounds of the scraping iron, sanding machine, hammer and saw, and the smell of paint, rope, and the damp spring fragrance of the nearby shore are just right. What work he has to do is a labor of love, for by doing it he not only gets to know his boat more intimately, but her transformation into a clean, shining beauty, and finally her launching, is an act of creation that properly reaffirms the spring season.

There are some men who complain about fitting out as a nuisance, a lot of toil and trouble. Usually this is in trying to explain to their wives the amount of time they spend in the boatyard. It may be a sly way of luring some friends or potential summer guests into the yard to show them the secret joys they might be missing; or it could just

Fifty years ago, a yacht club was strictly a masculine retreat, and ladies and children were allowed on the premises only on one or two special days during the year. Such an occasion was Ladies Day at the Larchmont (New York) Yacht Club when, as this picture shows, wives and families gathered to see the spectacle as the yachts got under way and sailed out of the harbor to race.

Things are different now. The ladies and the kids are an integral part of yacht club life, and instead of looking on they sail. This is the same lawn, looking out from the club porch one day during a recent Race Week while the crews were "making up" light sails and getting ready to go out and race.

The model room of the New York Yacht Club displays on its walls the greatest collection of half-models of yachts, covering well over a century of the sport's history, gathered together anywhere in the world. The ornate fireplace was imported from Italy when the clubhouse at 37 West 44th Street, New York, was built in 1901. A few of the club's great collection of trophies are shown on the table.

Until recent years, the New York Yacht Club maintained on the East River at 26th Street, handy to both the downtown financial district and the mid-town clubhouse, a landing. Many of its members, in summer, commuted from their homes in Long Island, Westchester, Connecticut and New Jersey, in their own boats, such as those shown in this 1924 photograph.

Not all yacht club houses and landings are as elaborate as those of the New York and Larchmont clubs. Here is the home of the Rockport (Mass.) Yacht Club, a very busy place in the summer.

After the racing, the pay-off. An important series of races has ended, and the Commodore is handing out the prizes while the contestants gather round to applaud the winners.

A modern development, used both for permanent moorings and for a home-away-from-home for the wandering cruiser, is the "marina." Largest of them all, so far, is Bahia Mar, maintained by the city of Fort Lauderdale, Florida, which accommodates several hundred yachts in its slips. It offers the cruiser such conveniences as running fresh water, city electrical power, grocery delivery service, garbage collection, restaurant, bar and parking lot, not to mention an ocean bathing beach just across the road.

be that these chronic grousers are so spoiled and lazy they would even complain about climbing the few steps that lead through the pearly gates.

To the majority of people who get afloat, boating means going fishing. In Florida it can mean going after leaping tarpon in a narrow, glassy stream in the lush Everglades, or after wily bonefish on the shallow coastal flats. Off the sandy coast, king mackerel put up a good fight on light tackle, while out in the rolling blue Gulf Stream deep-sea fishermen stalk marlin and tuna. They troll for striped bass in the surf off Montauk Point, and bottom-fish for cod offshore in the Atlantic. A green Wisconsin lake hides the big-mouthed muskellunge, and the brown Mississippi, the lazy catfish. There is drift fishing in the Ozarks and the Salmon Derby of the Pacific Northwest.

Fishing boats are as different as fish. A luxury, deep-sea sport fisherman, forty-five feet in length, equipped with two 250-horse-power engines, depth recorder, ship-to-shore phone, radio direction finder, automatic pilot, chrome-plated bar and the latest in fishing gear may cost $70,000. An outboard-powered skiff may cost $700. They each serve a different purpose, but from either a fisherman can try his luck with a simple hook and line or with the most complicated gadgetry in rods, reels, and lures.

The big, compact outboard motor can hurry a sturdy fishing boat to the fishing grounds, or it can give the speed addict, the water-borne hot rodder and the aquatic athlete plenty of thrills and exercise. In a high-speed, two-tone, upholstered runabout the feeling of speed is immediate. There is the swish of rushing water and the cool flick of flying spray. The lift and fall of the racing hull bring the surge of power so close that the quivering sensation of speed is felt on all sides, through the feet, seat and finger tips.

Behind these speedy little craft, the sight of a water skier, whipping along in the white wake, or swooping in wide S curves through it, is a part of the scenery all across the nation. For a time, in their enthusiasm with a new and active sport, it seemed as though the nautical hot rods would prove a serious safety hazard and general nuisance around crowded waters. Educational programs, however, stressing safety and courtesy afloat, have been launched by organizations and publications interested in the sport, from the boating industry and the United States Coast Guard. They have already had a moderating effect, and their continuance can only be a benefit to all.

In yachting, independence and self-reliance are most important factors. It is logical then, that where considerations of safety affect other craft and people, much of the control necessary should come through self-discipline. A fine example of this kind of action is shown in the work of the members of the United States Power Squadrons, in providing classes for persons interested in acquiring new knowledge and skills in boating. The United States Coast Guard Auxiliary through its members, provides facilities for the voluntary inspection of craft to be sure they meet the legal requirements of safety.

The development of powerful outboard motors led to their use on larger boats, and within the past few years the outboard cruiser has been highly refined. Large enough to be slept in comfortably, light enough to be towed on a trailer behind an auto, it opens up new cruising grounds all around the country. Between the larger cruisers and the variety of smaller craft towed on them, the trailer makes the driveway behind the house the starting point of water-borne adventure in all directions of the compass. The would-be sailor no longer has to live near the water. With his boat on a trailer, the lake a hundred miles distant is only a few hours away. He does not even have to wait for the spring thaw. In the winter, trailer-towed boats stream in a steady procession from the snow-covered North to the sunny South. A great number of people thus enjoy winter boating who might otherwise be limited by reason of finance or leisure time.

For the larger yachts, the annual trip south has been common for a long time. Like the birds, each year there is a migration numbering in the thousands down the East Coast, and from the Great Lakes down the Mississippi to Florida. Many yachts serve as winter homes afloat. A few of the sailboats enter the winter racing events. Some are kept there, just waiting and available to their owners and their friends for vacations through the winter season.

The large, publicly financed marinas, and the thousands of privately built docks are just about keeping up with the demand for their facilities, particularly near the larger cities; but many more will certainly be built. If the rapid growth of interest in boating is any indication of a trend, it is the way a lot of people want to spend their leisure time. We are just at the threshold of an age of automation in industry, with its promise of shorter work weeks and more leisure. It is a promise that for many people will find a good part of its fulfillment afloat.

One of the most important things the yacht clubs are doing today is teaching their boys and girls to sail, with well organized instruction programs. Here, the instructor shows his pupils, on the float of the American Yacht Club, a basic point of seamanship.

Having had their "skull practice" ashore, a couple of the girls make sail on their Blue Jay Class 14-foot sloop.

Here they go out to race, with their sails properly trimmed for beating to windward.

One of the last big steam yachts was J. P. Morgan's *Corsair*, silhouetted here against the sunset glow. Built in 1930, she was 343 feet long, steam-turbine-electric-driven. *Corsair* served in the British Navy through World War II. Later she became a commercial cruise ship and was finally wrecked on the Mexican Coast. The smaller power cruiser is Junius S. Morgan's *Shuttle,* while in the background are the America's Cup defender *Rainbow* and an unidentified schooner.

Two generations of yachting leaders. J. P. Morgan (right) and his son Junius S. Morgan, both famous as yacht owners and racing skippers, were commodores of the New York Yacht Club in 1919–21 and 1933–35 respectively. Their father and grandfather, the elder J. Pierpont Morgan, may possibly have made the remark often attributed to him, "If you have to ask what it costs to run a yacht, you can't afford one."

A magnificent sight, with her nearly 36,000 square feet of sail set, was the *Sea Cloud,* one of the few yachts ever rigged as a four-masted bark. She even set a skysail on her mainmast. She was designed by Cox and Stevens of New York, built in Germany in 1931, and was 316 feet long. She had diesel-electric auxiliary engines of 579 hp, and it took a crew of close to 40 sailors to handle her properly. When this picture was taken she was owned by Joseph P. Davies.

Another big auxiliary yacht was the three-masted schooner *Migrant*, 223 feet long. Just to shift headsails on her was a job that called for a lot of men out on the bowsprit. She was owned by Carll Tucker and was built by Lawley in 1929 from Gielow designs. She spread over 19,000 square feet of sail.

The yachtsmen of today, who *do* have to ask what it costs to run a yacht, find they can afford it all the same. Visit a yacht yard any spring and you'll see how. They do a good many of the fitting-out jobs themselves, and get a lot of enjoyment out of it too, and satisfaction in a good job well done. Whether it's sanding down topsides or paying seams, it's all part of the fun for enthusiastic boat owners and their families.

Yachts run smaller nowadays. This 65-foot diesel
yacht provides comfortable living quarters for half
a dozen in the owner's party and will make close to
20 knots. Modern equipment such as the radar
(seen above upper deck), radio telephone, deep
freeze and other handy gadgets of the electronic
age are luxuries even the big steam yachts of yes-
teryear didn't have.

Racers and cruisers constitute only a fraction of the yachting
population. There's the sport fisherman, like these men bound
out around stormy Montauk Point for a go at the tuna or whatever happens to be running at the time.

New on the pleasure-boating scene in the past few years is
the water ski enthusiast, gliding gracefully along in tow of
a fast inboard or outboard motorboat.

One of today's new developments in the yachting line is amphibious boating. With a modern trailer you can keep your boat in your own back yard, even if it's a hundred miles from the nearest water. You can have a summer boating vacation in Maine, or the Pacific Northwest, or on the Great Lakes, and a winter vacation in Florida, or southern California, or along the Gulf Coast.

Of course the amphibious idea isn't quite as new as some people would have us think. Back in 1866, Captain John Macgregor moved his canoe *Rob Roy* from one body of water to another by trailer, too, though his motive power wasn't quite up to Detroit's 1957 standards of speed and horsepower.

Or if you don't crave any of the foregoing forms of sport afloat, you can rendezvous with your friends in some calm, secluded harbor, along the coast or up some inland river.

Fun for all ages. A typical weekend scene that is duplicated in hundreds of places along the coasts, and for that matter throughout the country wherever there is usable boating water.

A record fleet for an ocean race, up to this writing, was the
fleet of 233 yachts that sailed in the race from Los Angeles
Harbor down the coast to Ensenada, Mexico, in May, 1957.
This is only a part of that fleet, taken at the start. The race had
a rare ending, for the smallest boat of the whole 233, the 24-
foot cutter *Renegade*, won the race on corrected time. Some of
her rivals were 90-footers.

Cruising yachtsmen of southern California aren't as lucky as those of New England, or Chesapeake Bay, or Puget Sound, in having an infinite number of good, snug harbors within easy reach. But they take full advantage of those they do have. This is a cove on Catalina Island, on a weekend with the fleet in from the Los Angeles sector of the mainland.

These International One-Design Class sloops, running off under spinnakers on the white-capped, sun-washed waters of Long Island Sound, typify one of the thrills of sailboat racing.

Even more exciting is a start of the same class,
beating into a strong head wind and a choppy sea,
with the boats sometimes only inches apart.

facing page:
A contrast to the light racing craft is the modern motor-sailer, a full-powered vessel but with a sailing rig that makes her a real "50–50." Most motor-sailors motor a good deal more than they sail, but some, like *Westerly,* spread light canvas and occasionally even sail in races. *Westerly* is a 79-foot over all ketch with General Motors diesels, designed by Sparkman and Stephens and built by Irving Jakobson in 1940. She served in the wartime Coast Guard patrol.

left:
Time to come about. The boys in Comet No. 3020 will never get across the bow of the bigger sloop on the starboard tack with the right of way.

below:
Canoe sailors have to be acrobats as well as seamen. Without the skipper's weight out on the end of that slide, she'd flop over in a minute. Canoes often do, but they have watertight decks, and the canoeman just gets them on their feet again and keeps on going.

Cruiser and racer. This husky cruising sloop stands up easily, with her big genoa jib on, to a breeze that has the little racing sloop down to her deck edge and her crew perched up on the weather deck.

One of the most famous of the New York Thirty-twos is Number 17. She was originally *Revonoc,* owned by Harvey Conover, and now is *Mustang,* owned by Roderick Stephens, Jr., one of the firm of Sparkman and Stephens which designed these 45-foot over all, 32-foot waterline sloops. Under both skippers, she has won many ocean and coastwise races over the past twenty years.

Nobody has more fun than a couple of boys in a boat, as you can tell by the grins on these two youngsters of the American Yacht Club junior sailing class.

Among small boat racing sailors today, the planing-type boat, of which this Thistle Class sloop is an example, is growing fast in popularity. Skillfully sailed in fresh breezes, they can be made to partly lift out of the water and skip along at speeds that take them past much larger conventional craft.

Mustang and the others of her class were built in the modern way. When a number of boats of the same design are to be built, a form or "jig" of correct shape is carefully built up and secured upside down on the shop floor. Over the jig, the stem, keel, sternpost and horn timber (the "backbone" of the hull) are set up; the ribs of steamed oak bent and secured, and the planking then cut and fastened to the frames. The upsidedown method saves many hours in hull construction. When planked, the hull is turned over and placed on its lead keel and the deck and interior built in.

These photos taken during the building of the New York Yacht Club 32-foot one-design class at the Nevins yard on City Island, N.Y., in 1936.

The newest method of yacht construction is molding of fiber-glass reinforced plastic. Laying up the hull in the female hull mold, the fiberglass is rolled on from the overhead roller. One half of the hull is laid up at one time.

The deck in its revolving cradle after it has been taken from the deck mold. The sanding and smoothing of the deck is done here before it is fastened to the hull. The deck is molded in one piece.

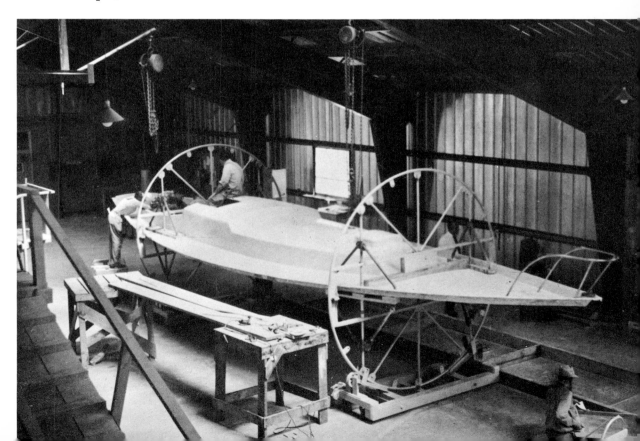

No yacht is too small to provide fun afloat. An 8-foot outboard-powered pram dinghy is quite big enough to take Dad and the girls fishing—as long as the weather is calm and they don't go too far out.

Close quarters on regatta day. You have to look out not only for competitors in your own class but for boats in a dozen other classes. Here are a Star, with the girl sailing, a 110 Class sloop and an American Yacht Club Bulldog all trying not to hit each other.

Squall making up. The big schooner and the other sloop have shortened sail in expectation of a butt-end-first gust of wind from under that cloud, but the New York Thirty in the foreground is evidently going to "tough it out," as the Thirties were famous for doing.

Compare this picture of a modern "Skeeter" with the old-fashioned iceboats shown earlier in the book, and you'll see that on hard water as well as soft, the boats have gotten smaller and more streamlined. But they are still capable of going, literally, faster than the wind.

The racing season never ends on Long Island Sound and a number of other active yachting centers. When the bigger boats are laid up in the fall, the sailors put their 11-foot "Frostbite" dinghies in commission and keep at it all winter, unless the harbor freezes up.

One of the spectacles of southern California sailing is the annual "Flight of the Snowbirds," when hundreds of these little sailing dinghies get together to battle it out for who's the champion.

The number of active yachtsmen has multiplied and remultiplied over the years, and still they come, as this scene at one of the recent National Motor Boat Shows, held in New York's Kingsbridge Armory, amply proves. Every boat on the floor, power or sail, dinghy or diesel cruiser, had its surrounding crowd of admirers, asking questions and looking, expertly or just covetously, over their attractions.

262

Acknowledgments

ALL but twelve of the photographs are from the Morris Rosenfeld file, supplemented by two collections acquired by him about fifty years ago from the work of the earlier marine photographers, James Burton and C. E. Bolles. To "Rosy's" devoted drive to pursue his interest of photography afloat, and to his intuitive sense of history, we owe the resources of this file.

The old prints and paintings are chiefly from the collections of the New York Historical Society and the Marine Association at Mystic, Connecticut. The portrait of Commodore John C. Stevens and the picture of *Maria* are from the Stevens Institute of Technology, Hoboken, New Jersey, and the painting of *Onrust* by Bollendonk from the Museum of the City of New York.

Special thanks are due Mr. Arthur B. Carlson of the New York Historical Society for his assistance there, and to Miss Eleanor Stephens, not only for her help at the Mariners Museum, but for her dedicated service to future yachtsmen, in preserving the collection of her father, the great yachting historian, W. P. Stephens.

The excellent photograph of Rod Stephens aboard *Dorade* was taken by his salty shipmate Porter Buck with a six-dollar box Brownie. The three recent Pacific Coast photographs, Snowbird Class start, Ensenada race start and Catalina anchorage, are Beckner Photos and the two construction photographs of the glass-hulled *Bounty* were provided by Coleman. The photographs of *Mayflower, Galatea, Volunteer, Thistle, Ella May* and *Oogrook* are by N. L. Stebbins.

The drawings of the old sloop, cutter, and *Gloriana* are through the courtesy of the marine architect Mr. Louis Kromholz, and to him a debt of gratitude is due for his shared interest in collecting old and valuable books on yachting.

To Mr. Stewart Johnson, of the publishers, is due my thanks for his extensive assistance and counsel.

To Mr. William H. Taylor I offer my deep appreciation for the joy of collaboration with a man of wholesome good humor and unstinting energy, tempered with the benefit of his wealth of yachting lore and experience.

To my father, Morris Rosenfeld, I acknowledge with gratitude his basic inspiration and guidance, and to my brothers David and William, the spark of their friendly rivalry and dependable assistance.

STANLEY ROSENFELD

The following illustrations appear by courtesy of the Marine Historical Society, Mystic, Conn.:

Harper's New Monthly Magazine, 1866, "The Cruise of the Rob Roy." The Rob Roy on Wheels, p. 571
ibid. Rob Roy in Rollers, p. 569
ibid. Esquimaux Feat, p. 569
ibid. Morning Visitors, p. 575
MacGregor, John, *The Voyage Alone in the Rob Roy.* 2nd ed. Sampson Low, Son, and Marston, 1868. The Rob Roy
Forest and Stream, May 8, 1880. Proa Ladronia
ibid. 1880. The Yacht Chipsa
ibid. January 1876. "How to Build Cheap Boats."
    A Fourteen Dollar Sailing Skiff
    A Twelve Dollar Row Boat
    A Five Dollar Skiff
    A Sixteen Dollar Family Boat
    The Fifteen Dollar Canoe
    A Thirty Dollar Yacht
Aquatic Monthly and Nautical Review, September 1872. Mischief
ibid. June 1872. Sappho rounding S. W. Spit
Loubat, J. F., *A Yachtsman's Scrapbook.* Brentano, 1887. International Challenge Match as published in *The Graphic,* London, August 8, 1874
ibid. Captain Bob Fish. Frontispiece
Oogrook by N. L. Stebbins
Ella May and *Lillie* by N. L. Stebbins

The following illustrations appear by courtesy of the New York Historical Society:

Fancy turning to windward. A section from The South Prospect of Ye Flourishing City of New York in the Province of New York
A section under the Dutch Church from the above
The Great Ocean Yacht Race, December 11, 1866. Currier and Ives
The Sail Boat. *Harper's Weekly,* August 21, 1869
The Great International Yacht Race, August 8, 1879. Currier and Ives
The Clipper Yacht, *America.* Currier and Ives
Yachting at the Helm. *Frank Leslie's Illustrated,* July 15, 1871
Under the Palisades. Fred S. Cozzens, 1883
New Bedford. Fred S. Cozzens, 1883
Sailing Race, Hudson River Canoe Club. *Harper's Weekly,* Volume XXIX
Ice Yachting on the Hudson. *Harper's Weekly,* Volume XXVII
In the Narrows. Fred S. Cozzens, 1883
The Fliers of the Atlantic Yacht Club, *Harper's Weekly,* July 30, 1887
Still the Champion. (Identified as Cat boat about 1880)
Cleopatra's Barge. Mott's *American Yachts and Yachtsmen.*
Yachting Fever in New York. *The Graphic,* September 21, 1901
Victorious Volunteer. James G. Tyler, 1887

Bibliography

The following books have been of particular use to the authors in their research:

Bradford, Gershom, *A Glossary of Sea Terms*. Dodd, Mead, 1942
Burgess, Edward, *American and English Yachts*. Scribners, 1887
Chapelle, Howard I., *The History of American Sailing Ships*. Norton, 1935
Clark, Arthur H., *The History of Yachting 1600–1815*. Putnam, 1904
Loomis, Alfred F., *Ocean Racing*. Morrow, 1936
Mott, *Yachts and Yachtsmen of America*. 1894
Olsen, Neils, *The American List Yacht*. L. H. Biglow, 1875, 1885
Stephens, W. P., *American Yachting*. Macmillan, 1904
———, *Traditions and Memories of American Yachting*. Motor Boating, 1942
Stone, Herbert L., *The America's Cup Races*. Macmillan, 1930
Sullivan, E., and others, *Yachting*. Badminton Library. Longmans Green, 1894
Vanderbilt, Harold S., *Enterprise*. Scribners, 1931
———, *On the Wind's Highway*. Scribners, 1931

The general files of the following periodicals and newspapers have also been consulted by the authors:

Aquatic Monthly and Nautical Review
Forest and Stream
Herald (New York)
Lloyd's Register of American Yachts
Motor Boating
New York Times
Rudder
Yachting

Glossary

Adz, wooden-shipbuilder's cutting tool with blade at right angle to handle

Aft, toward the stern

Ballast, heavy weight in or on bottom of boat to give stability

Batten, a thin wooden slat inserted in a pocket in the leech of a sail, approximately at right angles to the edge, to prevent the after part of the sail from curving inward

Batten down, secure hatches against seas coming aboard

Beam, width

Boom, spar extending the foot of a sail

Bow, forward end of a vessel

Bowsprit, spar extending over the bow

Capsize, upset

Cast off, untie

Cat rig, a rig consisting of a single fore-and-aft sail

Caulking iron, tool used to drive caulking into seams between planks, to keep water out of a ship

Centerboard, pivoted, flat, vertical structure lowering through the keel, to prevent a sailing craft from sliding sideways

Chine, the line in a hull, extending in a sweeping curve fore-and-aft, at which the frames of the sides and the bottom frames join at an angle; the fore-and-aft structural framing along that line. Flat-bottom, V-bottom, and arc-bottom boats are chine-built, but round-bottom boats are not

Chop, a short, steep, irregular wave formation caused by wind

Class, a type of boat; a group of racing boats of similar characteristics. In a one-design class, all boats have the same rating under a measurement formula, and race without handicaps. In a handicap class, boats of unlike size and rating race together on a handicap (time allowance) system

Clew, the lower corner of a sail; in fore-and-aft sails, the lower after corner only. To clew-up is to lift the lower part of a sail, as for furling or to clear the rigging when tacking

Clipper ship, very fast, square-rigged, ocean-going sailing cargo vessel, especially of the 1840–1860 period

Closed course race, a race around buoys, starting and finishing at the same point, usually short enough to be sailed in an afternoon's racing

Cod head and mackerel tail, description of a vessel broad and bulky at the bow, tapering to slim lines aft

Concave bow, one with concave lines at the extreme forward part of the waterline

Corrected time, elapsed time made in a race, corrected by deducting the time allowance, if any

Craft, a boat or vessel

Cruising Club Rule, a formula for calculating the potential speed of a yacht, for handicapping (time allowance) purposes. It is a complicated rule filling a 15-page booklet

Cutter, a fore-and-aft rigged, one-masted sailing vessel with two or more headsails forward of the mast. Traditionally, a narrow, deep, heavy, plumb-stemmed hull having this type of rig

Double head-rig, a rig with two headsails (jib and forestaysail) forward of the mast

Draft, depth of a vessel from the waterline to the extreme low point; i. e. "She drew (had a draft of) seven feet"

Fin keel, a platelike structure extending below the structural keel of the hull, carrying ballast at its lower edge

Fittings, equipment; hardware

Foresail, the sail hoisted on the forward mast of a schooner. (Sometimes used for "forestaysail" in a cutter)

Forestaysail, the triangular headsail just forward of the mast, in a vessel having two or more headsails. The sail forward of it is the jib

Genoa jib, a very large single headsail, the after part of which overlaps the mast by a considerable distance

Gunter rig, a triangular sail with a gaff which, when hoisted, stands parallel to and close against the mast

Hatches, openings in the deck of a vessel

Headsails, all sails set forward of the foremost mast

Heel, to incline laterally; to "tip"

Helm, steering apparatus

Hollow bow, *see* concave bow

Housing bowsprit, one that can be slid in and out along the deck

Hull, the whole solid structure of a vessel, excluding rig, spars, engines, equipment, hatch covers, rudder, etc.

Inboard, not extending outside the bow, stern or sides

International Rule, one of the many rules for measuring yachts for rating (handicap) purposes

Jib, the sail forward of the mast when a boat has only one sail there; otherwise, the second headsail forward of the mast

Jib-headed rig, one in which the sails hoisted on the masts, such as mainsail, foresail, mizzen, etc., are triangular in shape coming to a point at the masthead

Keel yacht, one whose hull structure is quite deep, providing good lateral plane

Ketch, a two-masted, fore-and-aft-rigged vessel; the taller mast is the forward one; the shorter mast is stepped aft, but still forward of the after end of the waterline

Lateral plane, a vessel's broadside, underwater profile; it provides resistance to sidewise motion, making it possible to sail across or into the wind in-instead of just blowing off before it

Lee, direction toward which the wind is blowing

Leeboards, pivoted, flat, vertical structures, sliding up and down each side of a vessel. When lowered into the water they provide lateral planes, substituting for centerboard or keel

Leech (or leach), the after edge of a fore-and-aft sail; in a square sail, both vertical edges are sometimes called leeches

Leeward, toward the lee

Leg of a course, straight part of a race course between two buoys or other turning points

Log, apparatus for determining the speed a vessel is traveling; to log 10 knots is to go through the water at 10 nautical miles an hour. Also, a notebook or other record of everything that goes on aboard ship

Luff, to change course into the wind, so that the sails shake and, if the luff is held, headway stops; also, the leading edge of a sail

Lugsails, a four-sided, fore-and-aft sail, with a yard along its head; the forward part of the sail and yard extend forward of the mast. (But "to lug sail" means to carry too much canvas in a strong wind)

Mainsail, principal working sail of a yacht, always hoisted on a mast. In a sloop or cutter, set on the only mast; in a yawl or ketch, on the forward mast; in a schooner, on the after mast (or second mast if she has more than two)

Marconi rig, *see* jib-headed rig

Mast track, metal strip down the after side of a mast, to which the sail is attached by metal slides

Match race, a race between two yachts

Meter-boats, yachts built to the International Rule of Measurement are classified by their rating expressed in meters, i. e., 6-meter, 12-meter, etc.

Midships (amidships), the center line fore and aft over the keel, or the central part of a vessel, midway between bow and stern

One-design class, one in which all boats are identical in design and construction

Overhang, the part of a hull extending above water forward of the forward end of the waterline or abaft the after end of the waterline

Packet, a vessel carrying passengers; commonly applied to square-rigged sailing vessels

Parachute spinnaker, a very large, light spinnaker, developed since about 1930

Pilot boat, a small vessel used to put pilots aboard inbound ships and take them off outward-bounders

Pram, a small, light, rowing, sailing or outboard-powered dinghy, square at both ends

Put the helm up, to bear off, or change course to leeward, away from the direction from which the wind blows

Restricted class, a racing class in which some dimensions and characteristics are fixed but others are allowed certain variations within fixed limits

Rig, the above-deck structure of a sailing craft, including sails, spars, stays and ropes; to put a rig, or any part of a rig, on a vessel

Rigging, the ropes of a sailing boat's rig; standing rigging is the fixed part, such as stays and shrouds; running rigging includes the moving parts such as sheets, halyards, etc. by which the sails are hoisted and trimmed

Rudder, the flat, vertical, pivoting structure, usually hinged to the after end of the keel, by which the vessel is steered. It is controlled from on deck by a tiller or by a wheel operating through gears or ropes

Rule of measurement, any of a wide variety of mathematical formulae by which the potential speed of a boat is calculated, for rating (handicap) purposes. It takes into account various factors which make boats faster or slower, such as length, sail area, beam, draft, weight, and numerous other factors. Rules range from simple length-and-sail-area equations to complicated statements of measurements and restrictions which occupy 15 or 20 pages of printed matter. In effect, it is a speed formula

Sail plan, the design of all the sails which drive a vessel. (For sail plan of hermaphrodite brig see pages 74–75)

Schooner, a sailing vessel of two or more masts, with the after mast (or masts) as tall as, or taller, than the foremast. Schooner yachts are usually two-masted with the after sail (mainsail) substantially larger than the foresail

Scow, in sailing craft, a broad, flat-bottomed type of hull

Sea-kindly, said of a vessel which is safe, rides comfortably, and is easily handled under storm conditions

Semi-fisherman schooner, a schooner yacht of a type resembling the famous Gloucester fishing schooners, with certain refinements to adapt her for yacht use

Sheets, the ropes by which the trim of the sails is adjusted, from nearly flat amidships for beating to windward, to broad off for running before the wind

Shorten sail, to reduce the area of canvas exposed to the wind, either by taking down some of the sails or by reefing (i. e., rolling up the lower part of the sail and tying it in a bundle)

Shrouds, the lateral stays which hold a mast up against the side pressure of the wind; "side stays"

Skimming dish, description of a vessel of light weight and shallow draft

Skipper, the captain, or person in command of a boat or vessel

Skylights, coverings of hatches by which light and air are admitted below decks

Sloop, a single-masted sailing vessel with one or more headsails. Traditionally the sloop had one headsail, but in present practice the terms sloop and cutter, as applied to the rig, are used almost interchangeably

Spars, wooden or metal poles on which sails are set. They include masts, booms, gaffs (extending the head of a sail vertically), bowsprits, and spinnaker poles

Spinnaker, a large, light sail set forward of the mast and boomed out with a spinnaker pole, used for running before the wind or reaching with the wind anywhere abaft the beam

Stern, the back end of a vessel

Taffrail, the rail across the stern

Tender, said of a vessel easily heeled (tipped sideways) by light or moderate breezes

Tiller, horizontal bar bolted through the rudder head, by which the rudder is controlled and the boat steered

Time allowance, the amount of time which is deducted from the actual elapsed time made by a boat in a race to obtain her corrected time. It is based on standard tables showing second-per-mile for each tenth of a foot of rating, multiplied by the number of miles in the course. The highest rating or "scratch" boat receives no allowance

Topmast, upward extension of a mast, on which a topsail is set

Topsail, sail set above another sail such as the mainsail, foresail, etc.

Transom, flat or curved surface at right angles to the keel, forming the stern of a hull; also, a settee or berth in a boat's cabin

Trim sails, to adjust them to give maximum driving power with relation to the direction of the wind and the vessel's course

Watch, the period, commonly four hours, during which one part of the crew runs a vessel; the members of a crew who work together during such a period

Waterline, in length, the distance from the point of the hull where it enters the water forward to the point where it leaves it aft; the waterline plane is the shape of a vertical section through the hull that would appear if a model of the hull were sawn through along the surface of the water from stem to stern

Whisker pole, a short, light spar used temporarily to hold a headsail out on the side opposite to the mainsail; takes the place of a spinnaker pole in small craft that do not carry spinnakers

Windjammer, a sailing vessel; a person who sails one

Windward, the direction from which the wind blows. (Opposite to leeward)

Yawl, a two-masted, fore-and-aft-rigged sailing craft, with the larger mast and sail forward and a small mizzen abaft the after end of the waterline, differing only in this respect from the ketch

Index